Politics and International Relations in the Middle East

Dedicated to the memory of

J.P. Bannerman

(1934–1990)

Politics and International Relations in the Middle East

Continuity and Change

Edited by

M. Jane Davis

Department of International Politics
University of Wales

Edward Elgar
Aldershot, UK • Brookfield, US

Published by
Edward Elgar Publishing Limited
Gower House
Croft Road
Aldershot
Hants GU11 3HR
UK

Edward Elgar Publishing Company
Old Post Road
Brookfield
Vermont 05036
US

British Library Cataloguing in Publication Data
Politics and International Relations in
the Middle East: Continuity and Change
    I. Davis, M. Jane
    320.956

Library of Congress Cataloguing in Publication Data
Politics and international relations in the Middle East : continuity
    and change / edited by M. Jane Davis. — 1st ed.
        p.   cm.
    Includes bibliographical references (p.) and index.
    1. Middle East—Politics and government—1979–   I. Davis, Jane,
1950– .
    DS63.1.P673   1995
    956.05'3—dc20
                                                          94–45149
                                                          CIP

ISBN 1 85898 234 0

Printed and bound in Great Britain by
Hartnolls Limited, Bodmin, Cornwall

Contents

Figures

Contributors

M. Jane Davis is Lecturer in the Department of International Politics, University of Wales, Aberystwyth.

David Gore-Booth, formerly Assistant Under-Secretary for the Middle East in the Foreign and Commonwealth Office, London, is HM Ambassador to the Kingdom of Saudi Arabia.

Rosemary Hollis is Research Fellow, Royal United Services Institute for Defence Studies, London.

Derek Hopwood is Director of the Middle East Centre and Fellow of St Antony's College, University of Oxford.

Christopher Rundle is Researcher on Iranian affairs in the Research and Analysis Department of the Foreign and Commonwealth Office, London.

Greg Shapland is Researcher in the Research and Analysis Department of the Foreign and Commonwealth Office, London.

Avi Shlaim is Alastair Buchan Reader in International Relations and Fellow of St Antony's College, University of Oxford.

Charles Tripp is Senior Lecturer, Department of Politics, School of Oriental and African Studies, University of London.

Julian Walker is Researcher on boundary questions in the Middle East in the Research and Analysis Department, Foreign and Commonwealth Office, London.

Rodney Wilson is Reader in the Department of Economics, University of Durham.

Foreword

In March 1992, the Research and Analysis Department of the Foreign and Commonwealth Office and the Department of International Politics of the University of Wales, Aberystwyth, jointly organized a conference at Wilton Park on the broad theme of 'Continuity and Change: The Middle East after the Gulf War'. The quality of the papers presented to the conference encouraged publication of this volume.

The Foreign and Commonwealth Office greatly values contacts with the academic world and has sought to develop them. The Wilton Park conference was an expression of these efforts, which I am convinced benefits both sides: the practitioners of foreign policy and those who study, research and teach the subject at British universities. Each can learn from the other. The conference was particularly valuable to those of our new entrant diplomats who attended and whose career will be centred on the Middle East.

The conference also commemorated the work of the late J.P. (Patrick) Bannerman, for many years the head of the Middle East Section of the Research and Analysis Department, whose untimely death occurred in July 1990. His career spanned both the diplomatic and the academic worlds. In his later years, he had concentrated on furthering official understanding of Islam, a field which brought him increasingly into contact with the academic world, culminating in a year's sabbatical at the University of Virginia. That, in turn, resulted in his well-received book, *Islam in Perspective*, (London: Routledge for the Royal Institute of International Affairs, 1988), which made his work accessible to a readership far beyond the Foreign and Commonwealth Office.

David Gore-Booth

Introduction: Middle East politics after the Gulf War

M. Jane Davis

This book, benefiting from the perspective provided by the momentous events in the Gulf in 1990–91, examines a number of themes which promise to occupy those concerned with developments in the Middle East for the foreseeable future. While the Gulf War itself was a dramatic landmark in the history of the Middle East, only in hindsight will its true impact on the region be fully appreciated. The chapters in this volume provide a selective overview of issues which have come to dominate the politics of the Middle East, and which promise to continue in that vein. They do not purport to provide comprehensive and definitive analysis of the immediate post-war climate in the region. Rather they serve as a reminder of the extensive range of problems facing Middle Eastern countries. Some of these problems, such as concern over Gulf security and the creation of a new regional alignment, emanate directly from the events of 1990–91; others, such as the debates over water rights and boundaries, reflect established and continuing themes in the modern Middle East. Together they convey something of the political flavour of the region at a crucial period in its history. In doing so they emit contrasting signals in that they indicate both continuity and change. In this respect they confirm the difficulties involved in identifying what is permanent and what is not.

Assessing prevailing and likely future trends is hazardous in any context, as it is always likely to produce more questions than answers. To undertake the task within a regional grouping of states poses a variety of challenges, not least the disentangling of conflicting perceptions and interests which so frequently thwart attempts at objective analysis. Such efforts are doubly hampered when the region is simultaneously and inextricably caught up in a global transformation, such as the abrupt ending of the Cold War, which itself requires fundamental reassessment of long-established policies and key interests.

The uncertainties which abound when the international system is in an unprecedented state of flux, make predictability all the more hazardous in a region renowned for conflict and instability. Consequently, to attempt an assessment of present and future developments in the dual context of global and regional volatility, and at a time acknowledged to be a watershed both in regional and international developments, might be considered somewhat daunting – even more so when the region in question is the Middle East, where the nuances of political life and indigenous culture have served so often to defy the logic of external assumptions about the area and to frustrate expectations of objective analysis.

Lack of objectivity is a familiar and accepted hazard in the analysis of international relations. However, in evaluating political developments in the Middle East the problem is compounded by deep-rooted cultural antagonisms generated between and within rival cultures and civilizations, namely Occident and Orient. It is not diminished by the kind of passionate debates which typify and inflame most Middle Eastern issues. At times of regional crisis, cultural fault-lines only serve to highlight and exacerbate existing tensions. Equally, emphasis on the Occident–Orient divide distracts attention from differences within those respective groupings. Both have found it convenient – with one exception since 1948 – to define their relationship in terms of two allegedly homogeneous entities: the Western world and the Islamic world. Yet the reality is very different. This overly simplistic approach ignores the innumerable issues which detract from, and contradict, cultural exclusivity; and it promises to obscure rather than to enlighten.

There are some parallels with the former East–West ideological schism which, for the duration of the Cold War, suppressed intra-bloc differences and rival nationalisms. It might be argued that just as the Cold War suppressed latent conflict, its demise, together with the onset of the Gulf crisis, exposed latent pragmatism. Between them, the ending of the Cold War and the outcome of the Gulf conflict – the conduct of the latter being more than a little dependent on the former – have been seen as contributing not insubstantially to a seismic change in the conduct of international relations: the creation of a 'new world order' no less (see Buzan, 1992, pp. 431–51 and Roberts, 1992, pp. 509–25).

While there was much about the Gulf crisis that was unprecedented, particularly in relation to the nature of the political alignments, the role of the United Nations Security Council and the use of sophisticated weapons technology, there was also much that was familiar. After all, the war was fought to re-establish the territorial *status quo* and return to the kind of stability which had existed in the Gulf prior to 2 August 1990. It was not the intention of the coalition to dismember Iraq and create new political units as a punishment or in retaliation for the initial crime. Such extensive territorial revision would have destroyed the hard-won military coalition against Saddam Hussein and created new tensions and animosities. Ambitious changes to the *status quo* promised endless turmoil with a potential to unravel the entire political map of the Middle East, with all the implications which that held for Western interests: not least, access to oil. In such an event the anticipated upheavals would probably have embroiled Western states ever more deeply as putative guardians of the Gulf shipping lanes and, more onerously, of any fledgling political creations.

Western involvement in revising the regional *status quo* would, by definition, call into question the legitimacy of that *status quo* and provoke the kind of animosity against the West which would render all previous charges of Western imperialism tame by comparison. The prospect of unlimited liability associated with such an open-ended commitment could not be countenanced by Western states newly liberated from the confines of the Cold War, and whose publics eagerly anticipated the benefits of the 'peace dividend'. The hope was that Saddam's regime would self-destruct.

Not surprisingly there was a notable reluctance among states to be seen to challenge the sanctity of the non-intervention principle, even for overtly humanitarian reasons, lest in doing so precedents were set, the consequences of which could not be foreseen. There was little enthusiasm among governments to enter unchartered waters by extending the right of humanitarian intervention in international law and thereby risk their own security. Presumably, if nothing else, the 'new world order' had to be predictable: *plus ça change, plus c'est la même chose*. Admittedly the Western allies had little choice but to undertake a humanitarian rescue operation in northern Iraq. Even so, the *ad hoc* 'safe haven' policy to protect the Kurds was an unforeseen infringement of Iraqi sovereignty that went beyond the goals of Operation Desert Storm.

If the conflict itself emitted contradictory signals as to the likely nature of the post-war environment, it is hardly surprising that the region as a whole exhibited similar signs of uncertainty and equivocation. While the pre-war political landscape could never be totally regained, the victory against Saddam promised continuity as much as it provoked change, more especially in the short term. What for the West appeared to offer a historical opportunity – and certainly one not to be missed – for conflict resolution and the redefinition of regional relationships, elicited less than enthusiastic reactions from both Middle Eastern elites and their publics. Their responses ranged from caution and cynicism through to suspicion and even outright hostility. Indeed, the extent to which the entire Gulf War enterprise reinforced existing divisions between Arab governments and their increasingly radicalized domestic opposition was an unwelcome consequence for Western and Arab leaderships alike. To the extent that the conflict was interpreted as serving the cause of Islamic fundamentalism or Arab nationalism, as in Egypt and Jordan for instance, it represented an unquantifiable threat to political establishments throughout the Middle East.

Significantly, and as in most upheavals in the region, the Palestinian dimension loomed large. It seemed that, having chosen to sup with the 'devil' of Saddam Hussein, the Palestinian leadership in Tunis had made even more tenuous its people's aspirations for statehood. Indeed, Palestinians were forced to pay an unusually high, although not altogether unknown, price for their political predicament. Not only did they lose what credibility they might have acquired as *bona fide* negotiators in the Middle Eastern peace process, but overnight they found themselves outcasts, and worse, in many of their adopted homelands. Marginalization, expulsion and even slaughter by their fellow Arabs were not new experiences for Palestinians. What was new was the extent to which they suddenly found themselves bereft of the patronage and financial support from those Gulf Arab states which had sustained the Palestinian movement so long in exile.

All the signs were that the Palestinians were in a far weaker, perhaps even irredeemable, position at the end of the Gulf conflict. There was more than a hint of historical inevitability about the seemingly infinite capacity of the leadership of the Palestine Liberation Organization (PLO) for choosing the 'wrong' option. Likewise, past experience gave little hope for optimism that lessons would be learned from the most recent catastrophe. Yet just slightly over six months after the end of the Gulf War, circumstances were to allow the beginning of peace talks between Arabs and Israelis. The circumstances included the removal of the complicating hand of the Soviet Union in the region, and the discovery of American will after the defeat of Saddam and in the face of the continuing Palestinian uprising in the occupied territories.

It is clear, however, that the Gulf War itself promised neither a panacea for states-in-waiting nor for states-in-being. For the former, the Palestinians of course, their ultimate goal of statehood was advanced more by default than by intent – that is, in spite of PLO support for Saddam. For the latter, particularly the Arab states of the Gulf, the combination of the Iraqi leader's ambitions and the presence of the military coalition forces assembled on their territories to repulse him, threatened to erode their sovereignty, or at the very least undermine the social fabric of their societies. The influx of Western military personnel posed almost as great a challenge to traditional Islamic society and culture as Saddam Hussein posed to the Gulf's ruling elites. Paradoxically, hindsight may suggest that orthodox Islam, notably in Saudi Arabia, and the political structures which it underpinned, were affected more by the presence of those sent to defend them than by the threat from Iraq.

Just as the connections between 'intentions' and 'consequences' in any context can be less than obvious, or even non-existent, so the distinction between altruistic and calculated motivation in any type of intervention can be at best blurred, if it exists at all. Similarly, the history of military intervention suggests that it is the fate of outside intervenors to slide rapidly from a position where they are welcome saviours to one where they are despised invaders. Whether a matter of perception or reality – both being potent means of persuasion in any culture – they serve as a reminder of the significance of the immediate political environment in which intervening forces find themselves. The nature of this relationship may mean the difference between an intervention being judged a 'success' or 'failure', regardless of the extent to which the initial objective has been achieved. The experience of Lebanon, whereby the claim of the intervening forces to be neutral defenders of the legitimate government appeared ludicrous to parties engaged in full-scale civil war, will be remembered for this, if for nothing else.

American concern to recruit a broad-based, truly multinational coalition, including key Arab states, which would operate under UN Security Council auspices, owed at least something to the lessons learned in Lebanon earlier. Having been criticized as partisan and virtually neo-imperialist in their Lebanese interventions in 1982, the Americans understood nearly a decade later that there was an immediate need to legitimize what was clearly a Western-run show. Yet however meticulous the planning and preparation for Operation Desert Shield and Operation Desert Storm may have been, the local political milieu, if not exactly an unknown quantity, remained well beyond the control of the coalition leaders. Despite, or perhaps because of, its alien nature, the military presence permeated the immediate socio-political environment, thereby ensuring that nothing would ever be quite the same again. In other words the Gulf crisis and its inordinately unpredictable outcomes will be woven into the already complex agenda of Middle Eastern political life. Indeed it has all the hallmarks of being a crucial reference point for future evaluations of trends and prospects in the region, particularly in the medium to long term.

Whether or not history judges the Gulf War to be one of the seminal events in the encounter between Occident and Orient, the developments of 1990–91 have the potential to provoke radical change in the indigenous political processes of the Middle East. This is all the more remarkable in a region where traditionally such processes have been resistant to change. Political structures and ideologies have come and gone but, as Charles Tripp observes in his insightful and rigorous discussion of long-term political trends in the Arab states of the region, patronage and clientelism demonstrate a stubborn resilience.

Tripp sets out to assess 'the capacity of patrimonial systems to remain the foundation of social hierarchy and order in the Middle East'. Inevitably, he is concerned with 'the uses of power to advance or to protect certain interests'. His analysis implicitly recognizes the existence and, indeed, the significance, of conflicting interests and the role of power in resolving conflicts. He examines 'the processes of change and the conventions of political conflict' at three separate, though interrelated, levels: society and ideology, regimes, and state structures. Initially he considers the changes to social structures since the days of empire, and the ideological reactions to these changes, such as nationalism and anti-colonialism. While these have either vanished or faded, their legacies continue to mould Middle Eastern lives. They have bequeathed innumerable causes for dispute and disaffection. More recently the potential for conflict has been fuelled by the rising expectations of the increasingly politicized masses.

The second area of analysis focuses on the characteristics of the region's governing elites, whose political, and occasionally physical, survival depends on their success in creating a delicate balance between 'carrots', in the form of the regimes' promises of protection and provision, and 'sticks', represented by the regimes' monopoly of violence and instruments of oppression. Of necessity dictatorships rely on a variety of authoritarian structures which, combined with a 'moral climate or political culture' peculiar to the states concerned, aim to make the system tolerable for the majority of the population, and certainly preferable to chaos for those who come to feel that they have a stake in the system. In this way, key sectors of the population themselves reinforce the apparatus of social control. Autocratic rule is perpetuated where a relationship of mutual interest is translated into one of mutual dependence, and patronage is dispensed in return for loyalty. However, the rigidity of the system necessarily invites challenges, although most changes of personnel are confined to the ruling group. As a result disaffection may be a more manageable threat, but this need not make the outcome less violent.

The evolution of state structures as agents of change constitutes Tripp's third level of analysis. Notably he focuses not on particular states, but more broadly on 'the structures of territorial, economic and military power of the state as a particular form of organization'. Because they are alternately regarded by regimes as a means of domination, and by the people as vehicles of repression, they provide a pervasive and implicitly violent theme in Middle Eastern politics. While the patrimonial system of power remains endemic in the Middle East it is increasingly challenged by the state, as ideas about 'sovereignty, representation and identity' take hold and threaten to dilute, if not erase, traditional forms of power. Consequently the potential for violence grows as elites, in attempting to shore up their positions by whatever means available to them, provoke 'unforeseen consequences' which set in train a different set of problems that in turn need to be managed.

As the indigenous system of power, patrimonialism has sustained and indeed embodied the traditions of Middle Eastern society, but it does not sit comfortably with the modern state. If Middle Eastern elites had little choice but to accept the Western concept of the state, they have subsequently put it to good use. Now it is clearly the basis of their power, both domestically and internationally. But, having accepted the concept, Middle Eastern regimes perforce had to accept what came with it and the manner in which it evolved. In recent years the state has brought with it disruptive ideas which challenge traditional forms of power and threaten to displace existing leaderships. Not for the first time Middle Eastern governments are caught between tradition and modernity. According to Tripp, it is how they attempt to reconcile the two and try to retain control that will constitute the main trends in Middle Eastern politics for the foreseeable future. It is also tempting to surmise that regional order will be one of the first casualties as the two traditions increasingly collide.

Political adjustments of the type and scale of those envisaged by Tripp can only be protracted and less than uniformly applied across the region. Given that their evolution will alternately be hastened or retarded by regional events of moment, fundamental change promises to be, at best, piecemeal and haphazard. In this context the Gulf War is likely be seen historically as a contributory rather than a determining factor.

In contrast, concern to devise and implement a new security regime in the Gulf came hard on the heels of Iraq's defeat by the military coalition. Because the enthusiasm, and indeed the initiatives, for such a scheme came from Arab members of the coalition – the six states of the Gulf Co-operation Council (GCC), Egypt and Syria – and the United States, the prospects for its development seemed more propitious than might otherwise have been anticipated given the discouraging history of Arab co-operation. The fact that such a coincidence of interests occurred was remarkable in itself; even more remarkable was the provision in the Arab scheme for a formal Western role, albeit at a distance. The cataclysmic nature of the Gulf conflict encouraged perceptions of it as a turning point in the history of the Middle East and, by implication, suggested that what followed would be regarded as a new, more harmonious era for the region. The euphoria generated by the outcome of the war, particularly in the West, reinforced existing optimism resulting from the ending of the Cold War. The idea took hold that with the ending of communism and the defeat of aggression in the Gulf, almost anything was possible. But, as Rosemary Hollis makes clear in her detailed and instructive account of the efforts to devise acceptable security structures in the Gulf, appearances are nothing if not deceptive.

The similarities between the ideas put forward by President Bush and the first draft of the Damascus Declaration prepared by the GCC states, Egypt and Syria, raised expectations that a new regional security framework was indeed possible, and in the making. Even the reference in the Damascus document to an 'Arab peace force' based on the continued presence of Egyptian and Syrian troops in the Gulf did not seem overly ambitious in the immediate aftermath of the war. However, what promised to be an unprecedented step in Arab co-operation quickly foundered in the face of familiar Arab sensitivities. In fact, as Hollis notes in her conclusion, the high point of co-operation between the 'six-plus-two' occurred in the 1991 Gulf War, prior to the formulation of the Damascus Declaration.

As the initial enthusiasm waned so did hopes that the 'new order' in the Gulf would be significantly different from the past. Differences, not uncommon to other Arab forums, steadily eroded the high-sounding principles produced in Damascus. Discrepancies between intentions and consequences magnified, revealing an innate reluctance to depart from tried and, if not entirely trusted, at least familiar practices. The reluctance and ultimate refusal by the GCC states to entrust their security to their larger Arab brothers was based on traditional as well as more immediate strategic, economic and domestic security considerations. For the Gulf states national security requirements clearly outweighed aspirations for a new system of common – collective? – security which placed considerable emphasis on the role of Egyptian and Syrian troops and which envisaged a more distant 'over-the-horizon' Western defence shield.

From the GCC's perspective, Saddam may have been tamed for the immediate future but that did not remove other threats, notably that from Iran – the traditional threat to the Sunni Arab Gulf. To the bemusement of the outside world the Gulf states' priorities required that Iraqi sovereignty remain intact lest Iran take advantage of its fragmentation to foment wider disruption. Hence the West's ostensible concern for the fate of the Kurds, and later the Shia of southern Iraq, was hardly welcomed by the ruling elites of the region. Each was preoccupied with its own internal security needs and mindful of its status as a potential target for Iranian opportunism.

Indeed, the Sunni Arab elites were in an invidious position. Their vulnerability dictated that their need for protection outweighed their sensibilities regarding Western intrusion, but at what price? While security arrangements with Western states contained problems for both sides, the governments of the Arab Gulf states risked paying the ultimate price – their downfall. Ironically, the Western presence had the potential to provoke two very different, but equally calamitous, prospects for Gulf elites: either irresistible pressure for democratic change or the success of a radical Islamic movement. Western interests were also at stake, since successor governments of whatever ideological hue would likely be less accommodating, if not thoroughly hostile, towards Western policies.

On the other hand, despite the perils of the social, political and cultural baggage which came with Western defence links, by strengthening these the smaller members of the GCC in particular, and not least Kuwait, signalled their lack of faith in the Damascus Declaration as a forerunner to a permanent security arrangement. Consequently, as Hollis argues, its value as a forum for regional security, if not completely eroded, is much diminished, not least because even when an issue as fundamental as their national survival is at stake, Arab governments continue to demonstrate that they have more to divide them than to unite them. Hollis's analysis suggests that the true impact of the Gulf War on regional security will be appreciated only in the longer term when the extent of the changes to a traditional way of life, long in a state of flux, can be more accurately assessed. Nonetheless, the evolution of Gulf security structures illustrates a specific aspect of a prevailing theme: the inherent pitfalls in pursuing either tradition or change in the Middle East, particularly where territorial issues are concerned.

In the Middle East, as elsewhere, land and water are two of the oldest reasons for conflict. Of obvious intrinsic value, they are also both finite commodities and hence lend themselves to politicization. This is particularly evident in the Middle East where both resources have generated or nourished disputes and violence for centuries. The rivalry over territory and water which the cradle of civilization has witnessed has largely determined the history, cultural traditions and political map of the region. These two resources therefore have a dual role inasmuch as they offer both context and explanation for regional developments. Because they represent continuing threads in this respect, they provide important reference points in the political evolution of the Middle East, but they also have the capacity to sustain the momentum for conflict in the region for the indefinite future.

It is in this context that Julian Walker traces the historical complexities of territorial boundaries in the Middle East from the time of the Ottoman Empire. His emphasis on the historical explanation of specific border problems in the region also provokes related themes: notably indigenous patterns of social behaviour and the competing cultural traditions as between Occident and Orient. Clearly the entire Western concept of the state and its corollary, territorial boundaries, was alien to the Middle East. This became apparent in the 19th century with the initial European attempts to supplant the loosening structures of Ottoman control. It was even more evident during the First World War and the subsequent creation of the League of Nations mandates system. Although appearances may have suggested otherwise, this period demonstrated the innate difficulties of transposing the essential trappings of one cultural system onto another, itself inherently resistant to change – and territorial boundaries were among the most obvious of such trappings.

Despite the best efforts of the mandatory powers to replicate a European system of control in the Middle East, the region functioned at two different levels: the one, structured, superficially powerful and operating distinctly European processes; the other, largely tribal and operating according to local custom and the dictates of indigenous society. The fact that territorial frontiers were an anathema to the latter group only widened the gulf between the two. It also emphasized a distinction which came to haunt the later years of European imperialism, as it has most great power–small power relationships: namely that the ability to wield power and draw lines on maps – or in the sand for that matter – was not necessarily synonymous with the exercise of authority. As Walker reminds us, the 'East is where Allah, not man, disposes'.

However, lines drawn in the sand, or otherwise, helped to ensure that the years between the two World Wars left a potent legacy, especially where these lines coincided with ethnic divisions, as in Palestine and southern Iran. Also at this time attitudes towards the demarcation of territory and the delineation of borders, particularly in the Arabian Peninsula and the Gulf, began to accommodate the growing significance of oil and the strategic interests of the European powers. As a result the region became a patchwork quilt of rival territorial claims and disputed boundaries. As Britain discovered, attempts to mediate these conflicts were not guaranteed to succeed. Some territorial disputes, such as that between Saudi Arabia and Oman, were resolved only as recently as 1991 when the greater threat of Iraq prevailed. Others, including the Iraq–Kuwait dispute, remain a live issue, while yet others have become dynastic squabbles with little relevance for the majority of the populations. The Saudi–Qatari border dispute, which erupted into small-scale fighting in October 1992, is a case in point.

It might be argued that the Gulf War of 1991 marked the culmination of a process that had begun when nationalist forces in the Middle East first recognized that they could best achieve their goal of independence by adopting Western ideas. Their success subsequently encouraged them to compete with the West at the international level, and to do so, if not on equal terms, at least on familiar terms. The Gulf War suggested that the Orient had whole-heartedly adopted the Western concept of the state, even if, in reality, it was somewhat adapted to accommodate local interests and needs. If Saddam was acting like a 19th century imperialist, his potential victims responded by invoking thoroughly Western norms, including the sanctity of the sovereign state and the inviolability of state frontiers – both of which inevitably facilitated the West's decision to restore the territorial *status quo ante*. There is a further irony in that as the governing elites of Middle Eastern states have come to guard their separate sovereignties ever more jealously, much of the West has been distracted by the notion of integration. Perhaps the uncertainties of the post-Cold War world are destined to intensify the former at the expense of the latter as states become increasingly inclined to seek security in what is familiar.

Acknowledging various reservations about the creation and development of existing state frontiers in the Middle East, Walker argues that without them not only could the region be in a worse situation, but that their existence has helped to shape the development of Middle Eastern society. But as the legacies of empire – both Ottoman and European – continue to be played out on the Middle Eastern stage, the issue of territorial boundaries becomes more, rather than less, sensitive. Whether this sensitivity is a concomitant of the post-imperial era and likely to intensify in the uncertainty of the post-Cold War era, or whether it is a specific reaction to the impact of the Western nation-state system on the region, it will almost certainly signify a further erosion of the distinctions between traditional (Eastern) and modern (Western) cultural proclivities in the Middle East.

In addition to lingering problems over borders and land, Greg Shapland's chapter reminds us that the region faces potential conflict because of the scarcity of water. Egypt, for example, with one million new mouths to feed every nine months, possesses a constant need to irrigate its narrow agricultural band and to provide energy for development, yet both the Sudan and Ethiopia have similar demands on the waters of the Nile. Much the same could be said of Syria, Iraq and Turkey, which share the waters of the Euphrates and Tigris rivers, and of Israel, Jordan and the Palestinian territories, which draw on the Jordan and Yarmouk rivers and the aquifers of the West Bank and Gaza Strip.

In the face of such pressing needs, *ad hoc* arrangements evolve out of necessity, as did co-operation after November 1989 between Syria and Iraq, which, though governed by rival Ba'thist regimes, hoped to persuade Turkey of the common interest in establishing national quotas of Euphrates water. Yet the tenuousness of such arrangements is revealed when larger concerns of regional politics intrude, such as the

Gulf crisis of 1990–91 when Syria joined the Western-led coalition against Iraq. The situation remains acute for Syria, more so than Iraq, particularly as it is estranged not only from Iraq, but also from Turkey which accuses the Asad regime of supporting anti-Turkish Kurdish rebels. That water provides both one context in which larger regional tension occurs and a reason for future conflict is perhaps seen most forcefully in the case of the Arab–Israeli dispute. Arabs suspect Israel of wanting to retain control over the occupied territories and its security zone in southern Lebanon in order to offset its critical need for water, and thus it looms large as a complicating factor in the negotiations between Israel on the one hand, and Lebanon, Jordan and Syria on the other, in the aftermath of the Madrid conference of October 1991. Indeed, no untapped sources of water exist in Israel or the occupied territories, and the potential for conflict remains a constant feature of this troubled landscape. Yet Shapland also suggests that the sharing of water resources is not a 'zero-sum game'. With more efficient usage of water and irrigation, greater desalination, the importation of water from the outside and the move from agriculture to industry, co-operation rather than conflict is a possibility.

If both change and continuity can be found in the thorny concerns of border demarcation and water-sharing, Rodney Wilson demonstrates that, although 'economic frustration' played a decisive role in the Gulf crisis, the larger economic patterns that have prevailed in the Middle East since the beginning of the 'petrol era' in the 1970s have not been substantially altered. The eight-year war with Iran had depleted the national treasury of Iraq and put it in substantial debt to the Arab states of the Gulf. Saddam had hoped to reschedule Iraq's debt repayments and increase its oil revenues, but the Gulf regimes were resistant to increases in Iraqi production quotas while allowing their own over-production and the downward pressure on the price of oil. Saddam thus felt justified in his grievances against his Gulf neighbours, particularly Kuwait, but the gamble upon which he was to embark in August 1990 was to reap only further economic damage. Although both Kuwait and Saudi Arabia have had to pay a substantial price for the defeat of Iraqi aggression, it is a price which they have been able to pay. Foreign assets and higher revenues from increased oil production have enabled them to finance reconstruction. But an 'Arab economic predicament' and the resultant pattern of economic inequality remain a troubling element of Middle Eastern life. Despite talk of Arab co-operation, often in the past enhanced by the appeal of Arab nationalism, the divide between the privileged Arab states of the Gulf and the poorer Arab states to the north – principally Jordan, Palestine, Syria and Egypt, but also including Iraq – is entrenched. A monolith such as 'the Arab world' or 'the Middle East' thus obscures more than it reveals; inter-Arab divisions are often more important than Arab hostilities with supposed 'outsiders'. Indeed, in pointing to the continuity both of Gulf wealth and of economic difficulties in the remaining parts of the Arab world, Wilson raises the sobering possibility of economics-driven instability within the Arab sub-region.

To Wilson's Arab economic calculus must be added the challenges that an oil-rich, but also revolutionary, Iran poses to Middle Eastern regional order. Christopher Rundle provides necessary perspective on a self-proclaimed 'Islamic revolution' that has been vilified in Western circles since its inception in 1978–79. Despite the obvious discontinuities which characterize the replacement of the Shah with a *mullah*-based regime, the revolution has had little difficulty in institutionalizing itself. Elections to the fourth Majles were held in April 1992, for example, and President Hashemi Rafsanjani was re-elected to a second four-year term in June 1993. Many key individuals who retain crucial positions of influence in the mid-1990s had attained prominence from the first days of the revolution. These include President Rafsanjani himself, formerly Speaker of the Majles; Ali Khamene'i, formerly President and, since Ayatollah Khomeini's death in 1989, supreme leader of the revolution; and Ali Akbar Velayati, who has been Foreign Minister since 1981.

More problematic for regional order has been the continuity of Iranian foreign policy concerns. Although ideologically inclined revolutionaries believe that the Islamic agenda cannot be advanced through normal diplomatic means – it would be tantamount to 'carrying water in a sieve' – the Iranian government has shown little difficulty in adapting to the procedures of the international system or following conventional geopolitical concerns. Here again the purported gulf between Orient and Occident cannot be substantiated. Despite the vitriolic antipathy directed towards Saddam Hussein during the Iran–Iraq War between 1980 and 1988, Ayatollah Khomeini drank the chalice of 'poison' and accepted the cease-fire provided by Security Council Resolution 598. Moreover, if the regime once mooted an independent foreign policy aligned with 'neither East nor West', it has since the early 1990s adopted, in the words of R.K. Ramazani, a policy of 'both North and South' (Ramazani, 1992, pp. 393–412). Characteristic of this is the desire to extend Iranian influence northwards into the Central Asian region and southwards into the Gulf. Indeed, the Iranian purchase of submarines and missiles from several sources and the reassertion of Iranian claims to the Tunbs and Abu Musa islands in September 1992, first occupied in late November 1971, are noteworthy for the echoes they provide of the Shah's foreign policy. Unsurprisingly, *plus ça change...*

Lately purchasing submarines from post-Soviet Russia and attempting to negotiate a settlement of the conflict in post-Soviet Azerbaijan, the Iranians have long been conscious of the Russian bear across the Caspian sea. Derek Hopwood offers a lucid overview of the historical patterns applicable to both imperial Russia and the Soviet Union in the Middle East. Remarkable continuity is found in the Russian and Soviet desire for territorial expansion and the deployment of a similar range of policies, including the patronizing of clients and the use of threats and force. Both even espoused ideological missions, whether pan-Slavism/ Orthodoxy or communism. In this regard, as Hopwood argues, Soviet policy was a continuation of Russian imperial policy by similar means. It was not surprising that both regarded the Middle East as an arena in which they could maximize their own influence whilst countering the influence of rival powers.

Yet there were critical differences from the 19th century. As a super-power, the Soviet Union needed to take the interests of the other super-power into account lest tension escalate into unacceptable levels of confrontation. The intervention in Afghanistan from December 1979 contained such a possibility of spillover into a larger conflict. In the Soviet era as well, local clients often proved more difficult than overt enemies. Gamal Abd-al Nasser, for instance, was a welcome irritant to the West, but, less happily, he also imprisoned local communists. Furthermore, the Egyptian regime and later the Syrian regime were scarcely prototypes of anti-bourgeois proletarianism, and the Soviets' ideology machine needed to be fine-tuned to an area in which class struggle did not appear inevitable.

The collapse of the Soviet Union and the end of the Cold War explain in part the possibility of breakthrough in the most intransigent of Middle Eastern problems, the Arab–Israeli conflict. Avi Shlaim's contribution to this volume outlines the dramatic moment when the breakthrough occurred. The United States, victor of both the Cold War and the Gulf War, used its considerable influence in 1991 to bring both Arabs and Israelis together in Madrid. The Israelis needed to be pushed to do so, but the Bush administration, particularly Secretary of State James Baker, were not hesitant. The *intifada*, the Palestinian uprising, had since late 1987 shown the economic and social costs of continued Israeli occupation and diplomatic inactivity. But the Palestinians also felt the need to respond to the new circumstances in which the PLO had lost its main backer with the collapse of the Soviet Union and its financial support from the Gulf states during the 1990–91 crisis: the Palestinians of the occupied territories had become increasingly impatient with the *status quo*, and contacts had been established between the PLO and the United States. As Shlaim explains, the Palestinians dominated the political theatre of Madrid and seized the high ground. They were to descend from it as the bilateral peace talks became mired in details and as internal opponents of the peace process – Jewish settlers in Israel and Hamas (the Islamic Resistance Movement) among Palestinians – actively opposed territorial compromise. The Soviet Union may no longer be a complicating factor, but Iranian support for Hamas and opposition to the peace process cannot be ignored.

Like Madrid in 1991, the limited peace agreement of September 1993, in which the Israelis have agreed to withdraw permanently from the Gaza Strip and the area around Jericho in return for PLO recognition of the state of Israel, is a major and felicitous disruption to one dominant pattern of regional conflict. But this volume's discussion of the larger issues of land, water, economics and internal political rivalries both explains the persistence of instability in the Middle East and implies that further discord is unlikely to be avoided in future.

ACKNOWLEDGEMENT

I am greatly indebted to James Piscatori without whom this book could not have been attempted. I also owe a debt of gratitude to Mark Smith who has so cheerfully and willingly devoted himself to the arduous task of unravelling the mysteries of indexing – if not of the Middle East.

1. Long-term political trends in the Arab states of the Middle East

Charles Tripp

INTRODUCTION

There are hazards involved in attempting to identify long-term political trends in the Middle East, as elsewhere. One is the danger of 'essentialism', whereby whatever happens in the politics of the region, it will always be seen as the expression of some irreducible and ingrained characteristic of its inhabitants. Another is the danger of what might be called 'inessentialism', whereby prominent features of contemporary politics are extrapolated and projected in an unproblematic way, suggesting that the future will be a rather more exaggerated version of the present. The danger of both of these approaches is due to the fact that they contain, if not a grain of truth, then an attempt to grapple with a real problem of social explanation. If they did not, it would be easy to dismiss them. When trying to investigate possible trends and movements in politics over time, it is necessary to understand how certain preoccupations and norms of behaviour are transmitted through several human generations. Equally, it is important to study the ways in which presently observable forms of political thought and behaviour are likely to shape the future, without necessarily asserting that they determine that future.

In a general way, looking at long-term political trends in the Middle East will involve examination of the uses of power to advance or to protect certain interests. Precisely because the assumption underlying this idea of the political is the existence of conflicting interests and the uses of power to resolve conflict, a number of questions arise which will define the area of investigation. The first concerns the definition of interests and the imaginative construction of forms of self-representation, as well as of those others against whom particular identities and their associated interests are being defined. The second relates to the environment in which not only are interests being defined, but the means of pursuing them are being structured. In this respect, questions arise concerning the forms of conflict and the ways in which conflict is resolved. This is important, since the lack of acceptance of the manner in which conflict is terminated, leads almost inevitably to its future renewal, possibly in a sublimated form.

When these questions are examined in the light of politics in the Middle East, it is possible to see why both the 'essentialist' and the 'inessentialist' responses point to an area of interest, even if their answers are ultimately unsatisfactory. As far as the first is concerned, the important thing is to understand the ways in which identities and interests are transmitted over time. Clearly, this opens up the possibility that they are also transformed over time, such that whilst the symbolic geography may appear much the same at first glance, the meanings will have altered significantly for the participants. The processes of change are worthy of attention here and, insofar as they involve the structured uses of power to foreclose certain options or to persuade others of desirable outcomes, the political nature of these processes will emerge. Equally, and relatedly, the question must arise as to whether the forms of political expression in the present are the symptoms or the causes of the kinds of conflict which characterize politics in the Middle East (Carr and Dumont, 1985, pp. 5–22; 119–58). Thus an imaginative effort is required to determine whether the forms of identity and interest, and the criteria of success associated with them, are as permanent as their advocates must perforce claim. Or are they shifting and impermanent, either because symbolic consolations cannot for long disguise structured inequality, or because a new symbolic vocabulary, associated with a different set of values and other criteria of success, may emerge?

In this respect, there are a number of levels on which it might be worth looking at these processes and the developing conventions of political conflict in the Middle East. The first lies in the realm of ideas and their social context; that is, the focus here will be on the changes which have been and are affecting social structures and thus the ideological responses which they have elicited or which they are in the process of forming. The second concerns the regimes themselves, that is, those generally restricted and restrictive groups of individuals who have taken over most of the states of the Middle East and, in taking them over, have sought to make them the instruments of their will. This has quite naturally produced challenges of specific kinds which have often succeeded in changing the personnel of the ruling regime, even if they have not always, or indeed scarcely ever, changed the logic by which the regime rules.

This brings one to the third level of analysis, which is that of the structures of the state, as they have been transferred, adapted and transmuted in the experiences of Middle Eastern peoples. In this regard it is not primarily the fate and impact of particular states which is in question, but rather the structures of territorial, economic and military power of the state as a particular form of organization. The continuing impact of this upon those who see it as the engine of their dominance (or as the controller of their lives) forms one of the abiding themes of Middle Eastern politics. In addition, however, it is worth asking whether the state itself has a particular logic as a form of power which demands similar kinds of response. This introduces the question of interstate relations. Specifically, it is worth asking, by way of conclusion, whether, as a result of the trends alluded to in the other three areas of politics, different kinds of relationship, as well as different kinds of issue, are being forced onto the agenda of Middle Eastern governments, shaping their relationships with each other and with the outside world.

IDEAS AND SOCIETY

During the period when most of the Middle East was under the control of the British and French Empires, ideas of national community, of self-determination and of national independence gained wide currency among the growing political public. These ideas had suggested that many of the ills resulting from the incorporation of Middle Eastern societies into European empires and into the international capitalist economy would be cured once the Arab peoples gained control over their own political destinies. Perhaps inevitably, given the stretch of the Arab world and the very different histories of its inhabitants, as well as the state structures established by the imperial powers, divergent views of the identity of the relevant national community began to emerge. The idea of the Arab nation may have continued to exist as an ideal, but more immediate and local communities became the actual bases of independence movements. However, regardless of the size, or even the identity, of the putative national community in whose name the struggle against the imperial powers may have been conducted, it became very clear after independence that political control over their own lives remained as remote as ever for the vast majority of the inhabitants of the Arab Middle East.

The realization of this during the decades following independence was partially obscured by the heady rhetoric of anti-imperialism. It was also disguised by the apparently limitless opportunities for many which seemed to open up as the old social classes were swept from power and members of hitherto marginalized or simply neglected social groups took over Arab states from Algeria to Iraq. However, by the early 1970s, the illusion of control was beginning to wear thin. Economic failure, manifest injustice, arbitrary rule and defeat in war had alerted many in the Middle East to the failings of their governments. The insecurity, the bewildering effects of disrupted communities and the loss of personal autonomy were often little better under the new rulers than under the old imperial dispensation. The major difference, however, was in the size of the political public. Just as the growing engagement of a mass public in the political struggle had made it difficult for the imperial powers to sustain belief in the permanence or legitimacy of their rule, so the regimes dominating the independent states were faced by the possibilities of widespread social rejection.

Consequently, one trend which has become more visible in Middle Eastern politics as the expectant political public has grown, is the demand for answerability of the rulers to the ruled. The demands for a better life, for security (whether material, cultural or legal) and above all the demand for an unprecedented, and possibly unrealistic, degree of control have been, and will continue to be, constant themes of Middle Eastern politics. This is not, of course, to say that they will everywhere take the same form or that they will be articulated with the same strength. On the contrary, the size and the restiveness of political publics differ widely across the Arab world, as do the capacities of governments to handle the challenges which these demands represent. Nevertheless, as a theme of political activity and political conflict the demand by people for greater answerability from those who would rule them is likely to grow ever more important (Norton, 1993, pp. 205–16;[1] al-Jabari, 1993, pp. 4–15).

The more important it becomes – and the effects of this have already been noticeable in the Middle East – the more salient will become two questions relevant to present and future political conflict. First, the question arises concerning the nature of the answerability of the rulers: to what or to whom should they answer? Various responses have been given, ranging from 'the people', through 'the nation', to 'God'. These ultimate authorities then require definition, such that some method can be established whereby rulers can be held systematically accountable to the rather different political principles which they signify. These definitions and these methods provoke further dispute, leading to conflict and to the realization that agreement on the need for answerability may, indeed, be simply the beginning of political argument (Deng, 1990, pp. 596–609).[2] Nevertheless, the significant development of late 20th century Middle Eastern politics in this regard is the fact that this argument is increasingly one in which large numbers of people engage. This may not make consensual politics particularly easy to achieve and is by no means a recipe for political quiescence or stability. Old structures of authority have been thrown into question and new ones have yet to prove themselves.

This feature also creates very specific challenges for the governing elites and raises the second question: how do the governing elites escape the implications of answerability? Their own structures of neo-patrimonial power are based almost entirely on the negation of systematic answerability, although each is aware of constituencies whose demands it would be unwise to ignore. However, granting the resources which would satisfy these demands has been the prerogative of the ruler. This is a far cry from submitting to the principle that resources may only be dispensed and commands issued in conformity with some impersonal principle of authority, embodied in the idea of the nation or of God. Quite clearly, this would leave the way open for interpretations of the rulers' obligations quite at variance with their immediate interests and could mean the dismantling of the patronage structures so assiduously constructed and maintained. Equally pernicious, as far as the maintenance of such networks is concerned, is the possibility that the rights of the ruled will be asserted against the interests of the rulers – rights which will be the subject of multiple interpretations by a growing mass public, aware of those rights and of the possibility of asserting them.

In fact this diversity of interpretation and the claim to equal rights by socially differentiated publics has given the present rulers of many Middle Eastern states something of a breathing-space. The expression of different identities and of different constructions of community, frequently within the boundaries of the same state, has often sat uneasily with the claim to equal rights to the resources of the state. Conflicts over the definition of communal identity, or over the nature of the authority whereby the government should properly exercise power, have allowed oligarchies of one kind and another to play on the nightmares of communal or sectarian strife that arise. These restrictive groups have then sought to suggest themselves as the arbiters who will ensure that the conflicts among the various communities cohabiting the state in question will not break out into open civil war (for example, Qurneh, 1986, pp. 210–14).[3] At a time when the ideas of community are still fluid, but when many of the fears associated with communal identification are at their most vivid, considerable space for action may be granted to that group of people which seizes the initiative and promises order, even at the price of a large measure of repression. This in turn permits the group to exploit communal difference to reinforce its own patronage networks. The suspicion is, therefore, that it is helping to create the very conditions which appear to demand its existence. This would not be surprising, since power tends to reproduce its own foundations, but it is a disconcerting trend for those who are hoping, on the contrary, that the space for a civil society can be created in Middle Eastern politics.

POLITICAL REGIMES

In the general absence of any systematic answerability or democratic processes of account in most of the Arab states, the focus of interest and analysis has inevitably been the ruling elite. In common with oligarchies everywhere, these groups rely upon a number of strategies which help to shore up their power and to retain their exclusive control over the symbolic and material resources which lend meaning and weight to that power. At the same time, in common with other oligarchies in different parts of the world, they are susceptible to weaknesses and their skill is largely a function of how well their members can reduce their vulnerability to those who are waiting to displace them. Thus despite the fact that they wish to give the impression of permanence, stability and even, in some cases, inevitability, they are involved in a constant, day-to-day process which some might characterize as state management and others as political survival. Depending upon the regime in question, of course, and the circumstances of the time, this is not to suggest that they are always involved in a life or death struggle. Rather, these are primarily authoritarian structures of power which are susceptible to a variety of internal strains. However, they would all be equally undermined by any effective movement for the assertion of rights by those outside the ruling group, as well as by the systematic answerability demanded by those who would see the rights of the state's citizens genuinely protected.[4]

Given the fact that the restrictive rule practised by every government in the Arab world is likely to be challenged by the trend, alluded to above, of the growing demand for a measure of accountability, the question to be asked is whether the authoritarian structures on which the rulers depend are resilient enough to meet the challenge. In most cases it is obvious that the main instrument for the maintenance of the system is the repressive apparatus of the state, adapted in various ways to meet the particular needs of the ruling family, clan or group when confronting challenges from the rest of society. This remains as true of the republics as of the monarchies in much of the Arab world. However, it is equally obvious that, whilst control of the main coercive apparatus may be a necessary condition of rule, it is not sufficient to explain the resilience and political longevity of a number of the Arab world's autocrats.

In order to understand their success in dominating their respective societies for so long, one must look beyond the violence they are able to command. More to the point, it is necessary to understand the moral climate, or political culture, of the society concerned. It is this which gives political meaning to the use of violence. It is also this which creates the ideational and ethical environment in which the rule of the autocrat makes sense in some important ways for significantly placed sections of the population (al-Sayyid, 1993, pp. 228–42). Throughout the Arab world, two significant functions of the autocrat, whether king or president, recur in the discourse of power, sometimes articulated in the official propaganda of the regime, but as often as not articulated in the patterns of behaviour and collaboration which allow the autocratic system to maintain itself. These functions can be broadly characterized as protection, on the one hand, and provision, on the other (Qurneh, 1986, pp. 407–83).

As far as protection is concerned, it has been an unspoken and a spoken part of the rationale for dictatorship that the central figure of the ruler is vital for the protection of society from outside forces, but equally from forces of social division and discord within the state itself. The nature of the external and internal forces will, of course, depend upon the history and the composition of the population of the country in question, but as often as not they will be somehow linked in the demonology of the regime – a demonology which is never an arbitrary invention, but rather corresponds in some sense to shared values and prejudices in the society at large. Whether the outside enemy be claimed to be 'Western imperialism', 'forces of reaction', 'atheist socialism', 'Islamic terrorism', 'Zionist expansionism' or 'Iranian aggression', the charge will frequently be that they have an internal fifth column working at their behest.

However, even without such an external threat, in many of the newly constituted states in the Middle East (the societies of which are undergoing potentially disruptive transformations), the imagined threat of internal conflict is something which is plausibly played upon by the ruling regime. The argument runs that only the ruler and his firm hand stands between the population and the forces of civil disorder. Depending upon the make-up, and thus the potential fault lines, of the society, these will be variously portrayed as tribal, ethnic, sectarian or class-based in character. In some countries the memory of such partisan strife is all too vivid and is often associated with periods when there was indeed some uncertainty about the competence or the reach of central authority. It is precisely for this reason that autocratic regimes have found this to be such a useful chord to strike at times when demands for greater openness, answerability and plural representation are being voiced with renewed vigour. The suggestion is, of course, that if all are allowed to represent their interests equally and if government is to be held answerable to this multiplicity of interests, anarchy – or more accurately *fitna* (civil strife or discord) – will ensue.

Protection from dangers real or imagined is not the only function of government. There is also the crucial question of provision – that is, of the provision of the resources of the state to the population. In the public rationale of Middle Eastern governments, the principle of universal entitlement is something to which all regimes, regardless of their formal constitution, claim to adhere. In practice, the system for distributing rewards and resources works in a much more inegalitarian fashion. Whilst it may be true that a minimum level of provision is available to every citizen of the state in question, in all of the Arab states of the Middle East the truly valuable resources are distributed through networks of patrons and clients, reaching down from the very highest power in the land.

For the ruler, possibly the most important day-to-day activity is the servicing and maintenance of these networks, since without them his power would crumble: clients would desert to other, more capable or more generous patrons and alternative leaders would emerge to challenge him. The importance of this system lies in its ubiquity, its relative efficiency in relation to the goals it is meant to achieve and its extraordinary adaptability to the condition and form of the territorial state established during this century in the Middle East. This adaptability perhaps explains the resilience of patrimonialism in the Middle East and the capacity it has to reinforce itself. Power is used to restrict access to resources, some of which are then redistributed, but at the behest of the ruler, and are targeted by him at those whom he thinks might be most useful to him, or are too dangerous to ignore or whatever. The point is that there is no question here of universal entitlement or of rights. Indeed, such notions would negate the structured inequality which is at the heart of the system. Instead, there is an expectation that the ruler, or a client of his who has resources to offer in turn, can be reached if the proper forms of submission are observed by the supplicant.

One of the interesting aspects of this system is the degree of its social acceptance across the Arab world. In each country, it will take different forms, depending upon the particular customs and circumstances in which it arose. Nevertheless, its persistence, regardless of changes of regime, of explicit changes in ideology and of repeated criticism from within these societies, is a testimony to the very restrictive nature of power. All are obliged to become collaborators in this system of clientelist networks because these are the socially effective networks through which power and resources run. In other words, patrimonial practices are the most effective ones and, in being so, they not only foreclose and take over other ways of proceeding, but also engender their own rationales. The multiple associations of the word *intisab* are a case in point.[5] Where the conventions and rules associated with *intisab* are absent, open violence can and will be used to maintain the exclusivity of the system.

In such a system it is clear that rulers have considerable capacities to meet challenges of the kind posed by those demanding greater answerability. From the power and resource centre of a multitude of patrimonial networks, the ruler can ensure that there is a very substantial body of people who will have a vested interest in seeing the system perpetuated. For those who attack the privileges and inequality upon which the system is founded, the ruler can hold up the spectre of the *fitna* which would ensue if a more egalitarian principle of equal rights to all the resources of the state were to be put into practice. The suggestion here is both that a degree of inequality is the price for political order and that the right form of submission can open the doors of opportunity for every individual.[6]

Resilient as these systems have proved themselves to be, there are nevertheless forces at work which may serve to undermine particular patrimonial regimes, although whether the principle itself would be undermined remains a moot point. Two features in particular should be borne in mind when contemplating future political trends in the Arab states of the Middle East. The first is the question of the personal survival of a number of the rulers themselves and the degree to which it can be expected that their patronage networks, hitherto a major prop of their regimes, could be said to have created a constituency which would ensure a smooth and relatively peaceful succession. The second feature is the growing crisis of resources which faces a number of these rulers and the effects which shortages have had, and will have, on the structures by which they have hitherto maintained themselves in power.

As far as the first question is concerned, there is not much point in speculating about the timing or the nature of the demise of particular leaders. Much will depend upon the vagaries of fate and of their physical well-being. However, it is worth noting that a number of leaders across the Middle East have now been in power for 20 years or more and have ensured that the structures of power in their own states should emanate from their own command. They have placed themselves at the centre of networks of patronage, as well as of apparatuses of coercion, and the question which arises is what happens when they go, as most of them must do during the coming decade.

There appear to be three possible options, none of which bode well for political stability and all of which may, ironically, contribute towards the eventual appearance of a successor autocrat. First, it is possible that on the death of Asad, of Qadhafi or of Saddam Hussein, for example, there will be a bid for power by those former clients of these men who will try to maintain the system of privilege from which they have benefited. This will, however, be an uncertain enterprise. There is obviously, on past record, a strong possibility that without the unifying grip of the leader in question, factions will soon be at each other's throats, giving expression to hitherto suppressed conflicts and clashes of will and of interest (for example, Seale, 1988 pp. 421–40).[7] In addition, the passing of such a leader in a system so consciously centred upon him, may destroy belief both in the authority and in the deterrent power of the system and unleash forces of social rejection.

More particularly, these conflicts may give rise to the second option whereby those who are watching and waiting to replace the old dictators with circles of patronage of their own will seize this moment to strike. The combination of intra-elite strife and an atmosphere of popular expectation of change would seem to provide the opportunity to act for many who had hitherto been biding their time. This, again, is likely to be a contested enterprise and holds out the prospect of precisely the kind of social discord, uncertainty and violence which would provide the space and the rationale for yet another authoritarian figure to emerge, promising to restore order. It is also possible that the demoralization and the internecine conflict not only of the existing elite, but also of a number of alternative elites, would provide the opportunity for those who are determined to overthrow the whole system to make a bid for power. In some respects this is the circumstance which many Middle Eastern opposition movements hope will allow them to put their principles into practice, whether those be the principles of a liberal, democratic, secular political order, or of an Islamic state.

The problem for such projects is that the passing of the autocrat may be attended by such a degree of violence, as various factions battle for the succession, that there will not be much space left for those who do not themselves have violent means at their disposal. In these circumstances the authoritarian aspect of the revolutionary project will come to the fore, and may follow its own logic at the expense of more participatory, consensual visions of civil order. In some respects the role played by violence is significant in that it often marks the hiatus between the breakdown of one patrimonial system and the establishment of another. Not only is violence implicit in any exclusionary system, but the violence of some forms of social conflict may come into the open at those times when there is no generally accepted form of social mediation or state deterrence in operation (Dann, 1969, pp. 223–6).[8] Consequently, whilst one can expect the passing of the dictators to be attended by a degree of instability, one should not expect those conditions to lead to the passing of patrimonial dictatorship as such. On the contrary, there are a number of reasons why such instability may encourage not only authoritarian opportunists, but also a general social acceptance of authoritarian control.

Although much may hinge upon the personal survival of the authoritarian rulers in the Arab Middle East, there is a second feature of these patrimonial societies which could be said to constitute a trend in their development and, possibly, a threat to their persistence. This has its roots in the challenge of coping with shortages of the resources needed to service the patronage networks upon which the ruling groups rely. In the oil-rich states of the Persian Gulf, this is not a serious problem at present, although there has been some more realistic thinking about the management of resources which once appeared boundless. In other countries there has been a concerted attempt to increase the capital base of the society and to ensure general economic growth by measures associated with the *infitah* or the liberalization of the economy (Vandewalle, 1991, pp. 216–31; Perthes, 1992, pp. 37–58; Farouk-Sluglett, 1993, pp.35–49). The term 'liberalization' may be somewhat misleading since these economic strategies are devised by an authoritarian ruling group, dynasty or clan to take some of the pressure off them as – hitherto – the sole source of provision.

Precisely because this is the political and social context in which such reforms or initiatives in the economy are taking place, it could be said that they are generally intended by the regimes in question to serve two broad purposes, one short term and one medium to long term. The short term objective is to recognize and to reward the clients of the regime by granting them a certain freedom of manoeuvre and enterprise in economic life. The privatization of land holdings, the encouragement of private enterprise investment in services and industry, or the licence to pursue international commerce – these are the forms which 'liberalization' has generally taken, giving advantage in the first instance to those individuals and families who are well connected with the regime, or whom the regime feels are worth cultivating. One can see, therefore, that the so-called 'liberalization' is, in the first instance, a way of extending and reinforcing the patronage network which maintains the regime. It is a way of granting favours and privileges to those who have attached themselves to the ruling group, but it also increases the numbers of those who have a stake in the continuity of the system that has granted them such favours. At the same time, of course, it has been made clear that these favours are very much in the nature of gifts which can be withdrawn, as well as bestowed. Licences and permits can be revoked or delayed and doors which open for instant access to the top decision-makers can be closed. More crudely, depending upon the circumstance and on the country, those who have profited from the regime's 'liberalization' can be reminded that their fate ultimately depends upon how useful they are to the regime.[9]

The longer-term objective is, of course, to develop the country economically by following a capitalist path of development. In all cases of 'liberalization' there is an element of disappointment and disillusion with the record of the state socialist path of development pursued during earlier decades. Clearly there is a hope that somehow the productive forces of capitalism can be harnessed to the development of the society in question. This is scarcely, if at all, due to a mass conversion to the ideology of liberal capitalism. More plausibly, it has to do with the relationship between Middle Eastern states and the world economy. From this perspective, capitalism is clearly the dominant economic form. Its hegemonic position is underlined by the fact that its criteria of efficiency and institutions require that others conform or perish. Consequently, in the search for investment capital and for the kind of resources which will permit economic development, Middle Eastern states, no less than others in the world, must constitute themselves as attractive targets for such investment or risk being left out altogether from the processes of economic growth. 'Liberalization' is carried out, therefore, in the hope both of attracting capital and of creating sufficient growth to persuade the generality of the population that the government is fulfilling its function as provider.

These may be the intentions of the regimes and, given their priorities and procedures, are perfectly comprehensible. However, there is always the question of unforeseen consequences. Thus economic 'liberalization' may be initiated as a way of reinforcing authoritarian and patrimonial regimes, but it may set in motion processes which work to undermine the principles on which such regimes are based. Most obviously, genuine political liberalization would require observance of the rule of law, as well as the codification of, and respect for, property rights (and, by association, of numerous other rights) which would corrode the exclusivist, informal but effective patronage systems on which these regimes depend. In addition, an element of public accountability might be required to ensure that these rights were indeed being respected.

In the context of the systems established in the Arab states of the Middle East, these would be radical demands indeed. However, it is conceivable that those who made their fortunes through patronage and favour may want to protect their interests from future depredations by the regime. As far as political activity is concerned, one question which arises is whether such groups of individuals will ever constitute a sufficiently weighty and independent force in society to bring about major change. More important, however, in view of the potential advantages of existing regimes, is whether such people would be willing to risk precisely the kind of violent social upheaval necessary, not simply to displace a particular regime, but to uproot a long-accepted and deeply entrenched principle of power. At first glance, this would seem unlikely, although their dissatisfaction with the *status quo* may cause some of the rifts within the elite which could herald political changes of some kind. Whatever the outcome – and the depth, let alone the success, of the economic 'liberalization' processes are far from clear as yet – the logic of capitalist production has caused a certain dynamic to get underway in the Arab states of the Middle East, creating new social forces, new self-definitions and interests and, potentially, new sources of political conflict.

STATE STRUCTURES

Capitalism seems to have a certain logic of its own which shapes the possible futures of those who engage upon it and, indeed, of those who reject it, precisely because of its ubiquity and its success. In a similar, and perhaps related, way, the territorial state-form, with its attendant ideas of sovereignty and its incipient nationalist ethos, has come to constitute the boundaries of effective political activity, as well as of the political imaginations of most of those who would aspire to power, whether in the Middle East or elsewhere. As a system of organizing territorial, economic and military power, the Western state-form has been an engine of quite startling success for those who have success-fully controlled and harnessed the social potential it represents, when compared with other forms of political organization.

The power of the European imperial states ensured that the Middle East should not escape this form of political organization, either as a model for political behaviour or, indeed, in the shape of specific states established by the European powers themselves. Despite considerable resistance to the particular state divisions imposed upon the peoples of the area, there were many who appreciated the power which the state conferred upon its rulers. Inexorably, it became the main field of politi-cal conflict, as well as the shaper of the political imaginations even of its enemies. Consequently, during the struggles for independence of the Arab peoples from European imperial domination, the state became the prize for the nationalist elites. Having won that prize, it was clear that they were loathe to let it go. Increasingly, therefore, the political geog-raphy of the Middle East came to be dominated by a range of independ-

ent Arab states, embodying in their territorial and administrative structures European ideas of political organization.

However, the Western form of the state is not a value-neutral organization of power which can be picked up and used instrumentally. On
the contrary, it embodies ideas of legitimate authority and of an ethical
order which must, in some manner, affect those who would adopt the
systems and practices of the state. Specifically, the Western state-form
has been associated with the ideas of territoriality and of nationalism. It
was perhaps inevitable, therefore, that, as the various Arab states began
to take on an air of permanence after independence and as they became
power bases for particular groups or clans, so the logic of the state
would begin to shape the language used to legitimize the rule of the
state.

This is a process which has been intermittently underway since the
first definition of the states in the Arab world. However, it has gained
momentum and its advocates have gained self-confidence as the dreams
of a certain kind of Arab nationalism faded and as the centrality of the
state in the effective use of power came to be realized. Consequently,
one trend has been visible which is likely to shape Middle Eastern
politics, both within and between states, for some time to come. It is a
consequence of the emergence of state-based nationalism and, although
expressed in a number of different ways, it represents a challenge on
various levels to the patrimonial, authoritarian and exclusivist clans
and groups which have paradoxically – and unwittingly? – sought to
use it for the enhancement of their own power. In essence, the trend can
be characterized as the developing territoriality of the Middle Eastern
Arab state. In general terms, it could be said to take four interrelated
and dynamic forms which are likely to leave their mark not only on the
ways in which Arab states in the Middle East are governed, but also on
the ways in which they conduct their relations with each other.

First, there is territory as the defining element of the state in relation
to other states and in the international system as a whole. This raises
questions of cartographic precision and definition, the transfer of the
two-dimensional plane to the three-dimensional domain where frontiers are established and *de facto* as well as *de jure* power begins and
ends. Secondly, there is the question of territory and the right to the
natural resources found in or on that territory. The state is, primarily, an
organization of power, and the wealth available to the rulers of the state
is as much an attribute of power as is its population, its technological
condition or its military forces. Resource questions are, obviously,

intimately linked to the territorial definition of the state, especially insofar as there may be claims and counterclaims by neighbouring states to territory with resource implications. The associated conflicts are about the relative rights by the parties concerned to exclusive exploitation of such resources. In this sense, therefore, the debate about material wealth is tied to the first aspect of territoriality and statehood.

However, it is also connected to the third aspect of territoriality and statehood. This refers to the connection between territory and political community. In particular, the association here is with a state as an organization not simply of power, but of *public* power – in other words, a *'res publica'*, commonly held for the collective benefit of its inhabitants or, in this connection, its citizenry. The territoriality of the Western state-form is, therefore, not simply a demarcated zone on a map, or even a designated area of land, but also an expression of a particular form of sovereignty. Underlying its past development, and its present rationale, lies the idea that that territory is, in some important senses, held in common: it defines the limits of a community of equal political rights and its associated resources are in some measure the property of all, when used in the name of the state. The struggle to assert these common rights has characterized the political development of the Western state, with radical implications for the earlier dispensations and rationales of power (Gilbert, 1975, pp. 206–11). The impact of the assertion of similar claims in the Middle East is likely to be no less dramatic.

In part this may also be due to the related consequences of the fourth aspect of territoriality and the state: the connection between territorial and national identities. The Western state-form is not simply a territorial organization of power, but is also constituted and justified as the outward expression of a collective, national identity. The nation-state is taken to be the supreme form of organization for any distinct people, defined largely in secular fashion as the *ethnie* whose distinctiveness and self-consciousness as a people links them to the state-creating project. This project has a territorial dimension, however, and, as a result, territory and national identity are taken to be inextricably mixed. In order to reinforce this sense of belonging to a distinct place, the moral status of the territorial state is emphasized, with the suggestion that it demarcates not merely an assembly of people, but a distinct ethical community.[10] The important feature for those who would rule the state is that the territory in question should correspond exactly to the territorial extent of the state, either given or claimed, depending upon the circumstances. Anything smaller would lead to provincial fragmentation and possible secession; anything significantly larger might lead to takeover by alternative centres of power and other elites.

These are the aspects of the territoriality of the state which should be borne in mind when seeking to understand the ways in which the particular logic of the state shapes politics in the Middle East, both between states and within the states themselves. All four aspects are perhaps better described as processes, working at different speeds in different environments to shape the agenda of political conflict and the attitudes and expectations associated with it. At certain times, one or other of these aspects may be more salient than others and it may seem as if the process associated with one form or other is the dominant one, suggesting certain rules, procedures and forms of behaviour. As long as all parties agree to these rules and can continue to see any potential dispute in more or less similar terms, the outcome will be, if not exactly predictable, then manageable.

However, when these rules no longer seem to have the force they once had, or when pressures are at work domestically and regionally to break that consensus and to suggest a new game entirely, the forms of conflict will change, as will the chances of managing it. Equally, the degree to which there is an interconnection between the expression of the various forms of state territoriality will begin to create, over time, new demands and pressures on ruling elites who may once have thought they could understand and manage the disputes in which they were engaged. This is particularly the case, for instance, in the connection between the delineation of a common national territory and the assertion of common political rights. In other words, as various governments have discovered, the exploitation of territorial border disputes for reasons of political consolidation or expediency may have a number of unforeseen consequences, possibly making such disputes easier to initiate than to resolve. By the same token, territorial claims may be forced upon a government at inopportune times, as far as that government is concerned, because of the domestic pressures which may build up around the symbolic importance of a particular piece of territory.

CONCLUSION

Examining long-term trends in the politics of the Middle East, as elsewhere, involves study of the processes of conflict which take place over time, as established ways of thought and constructions of interest are challenged by those who would displace them. The outcome of the contest is not predetermined, since the perception and definition of interest, as well as the strategies devised by one group or another, will change over time, shifting the terms of the debate and the arena of conflict itself. It is in this respect that one should view the major theme picked out here, namely the capacity of patrimonial systems to remain the foundation of social hierarchy and order in the Middle East. There is, in short, a continuing dialectic at work, whereby patrimonial structures are indeed challenged, but those who operate them devise strategies for their survival using instruments which in turn create new challenges.

Looking at the Middle East during the past few decades, there can be little doubt of the extraordinary resilience of patrimonialism, regardless of the ostensible ideological coloration of the regimes concerned. Although it has created resentment and has frequently led to the overthrow of particular regimes, those who seize power generally find themselves acting according to its principles, even if the criteria for deciding whom to favour and whom to exclude may have changed with each change of regime. In some respects, the ubiquity of this system and its extraordinary adaptability have held in check the assertion of common citizens' rights. In order to make it effective, its beneficiaries must operate a system of privilege, based on exclusion and selective favour, but the groups thus selected can come from all regions of the state and all sectors of society. Indeed, the wider the net is cast, the more prolific the networks created and the more people become implicated in the maintenance of a system that seems to work to their benefit. The effect, however, is to reinforce vertical divisions in society, frequently sharpening the sense of difference among various groups, but also impressing upon them the fact that they benefit more from submitting to a common patron than from competing, in open conflict, for scarce resources.

This suggestion, and the material rewards associated with it, have been one of the chief weapons in the armoury of those elites which have sought to prevent the assertion of common citizens' rights. Such an assertion would, of course, confront the ruling elite with those they seek to rule as a powerful and undifferentiated mass. It is for this reason that the rhetoric of every challenger of established regimes tries to portray the struggle as one between the 'rulers', on one side, and the 'people', on the other. However, where there exist no structural and few cultural forms in which the idea of the 'people' can be represented, the old vertical divisions will persist. Thus the challengers will either be thwarted by general incomprehension or suspicion of their motives or, if they succeed in achieving power, they may well themselves be drawn into a system of patronage and clientelism for reasons of political effectiveness and, indeed, survival.

Nevertheless, once established, they can themselves expect to face similar challenges, although possibly phrased in an idiom more appropriate to the changed conditions of their time. In part, this is due to their search for the resources they will need to service the networks of clients which are the foundation of their power. In part this is due to the structures of the state-form in which they must perforce, operate. The former may require of them the encouragement of productive forces in society which then begin to formulate their own ideas of how the state should be run. The expectation of a greater share in political power as individuals' economic power grows is a process common enough in history. Equally common has been the demand, by those who constitute (through their taxes) the revenue base of the government, for a say in how that revenue should be spent.

For those governments whose revenue comes directly from the natural resource of oil, rather than from productive social forces, the challenge may take a different form. In these cases they may be faced by the increasing assertion of common ownership of those revenues by all citizens of the state in the name of which, and on the territory of which, the oil is exploited. In this manner the state itself, as a particular form of organization, will bring with it ideas of sovereignty and of representation, as well as of identity, which would seem to challenge the patrimonial system of power. This does not mean its overthrow. It does, however, mean the need by elites to adapt their strategies to meet these challenges, and it also opens up the possibility of their collapse.

Even where nothing as dramatic as this takes place, a constant vigilance, shifting and manoeuvring will mark the efforts by entrenched elites in the Middle East to use whatever instruments are to hand – be they ideological, economic or coercive – to counter these challenges. These efforts will, in turn, have consequences unforeseen by the elites in question which will require further ingenuity to evade. The continuing dynamic of this process, regardless of its particular result in particular cases, is the result of a general truth about the condition of all Middle Eastern governments: the state constitutes the basis of their power, both as an agency of social control and as a force in the international arena. However, the particular Western state-form which they are obliged to operate brings with it ideas of sovereignty and conceptions of political identity and representation which continually challenge their own, indigenous organization of power. It is the working out of this generally unseen, but potent legacy which constitutes, in its various manifestations, the principal trend in the politics of the region in the late 20th century.

NOTES

1. The whole of the Spring 1993 issue of the *Middle East Journal* is useful in this regard.
2. The constitutional debates in Iran during 1979, before the present Constitution was adopted, are instructive in this respect. Equally illuminating are the debates and conflicts in Sudan following the overthrow of Nimayri's dictatorship.
3. See, for instance, President Hafiz al-Asad's address to the 7th Regional Congress of the Ba'th Party on 22 December 1979, in which he held up the sectarianism of the Muslim Brotherhood as one of the main threats facing Syrian society as a whole.
4. It is significant that the Saudi Arabian grouping in 1993 which formed an association and petitioned the government, adopted the language of rights and, specifically, the liberal, individualist language of rights, despite the fact that the political beliefs of the majority of those who associated themselves with this petition are a good deal closer to a restrictive interpretation of Islamic obligations than to liberalism or individualism.
5. This is a word which means 'relationship' or 'kinship', but which also has associations suggesting that which is fitting or appropriate.
6. See, for instance, Saddam Hussein's reflections on politics, the state and the proper relationship of the individual to the ruler, *Al-Thawra*, 23 August 1986 pp. 4–5.
7. For instance, this was graphically demonstrated in the manoeuvring and confrontation which occurred between senior members of the Syrian regime when President al-Asad was rumoured to be temporarily incapacitated by a heart attack.
8. See, for instance, the events in Kirkuk in 1959 or the events in Hama in 1982, once the Syrian government security forces had been driven from the city and before they reimposed their control by force.
9. See, for instance, Saddam Hussein's rather blunt reminder to Iraqi businessmen during the war with Iran concerning the source of their fortunes and the obligations which this placed upon them, in Isam al-Khafaji, 1986, pp. 8–9.
10. Understandably, this was a message which Saddam Hussein sought to drive home to all Iraqis during the war with Iran. See, for instance, his speech in 1987, where he claimed that, 'Iraq is not simply a geographical entity, but is now also a will...No force is capable of reversing this' (Saddam Hussein, 1987–90, p. 295).

2. 'Whatever happened to the Damascus Declaration?': evolving security structures in the Gulf

Rosemary Hollis

INTRODUCTION

In the wake of the Gulf War of 1991, two sets of blueprints for Gulf security emerged. The one to receive the most publicity was outlined by Arab Foreign Ministers in Damascus and by the United States President in Washington at the beginning of March 1991, immediately after the cessation of hostilities. The other – a set of *de facto* arrangements – has taken shape since then, and has fallen short of the more grandiose plans publicized initially by the wartime coalition partners.

On 6 March 1991, in an address to a joint session of Congress, President George Bush defined the challenges which he believed would have to be met to bring peace and order to the Middle East. In Damascus, meanwhile, the Foreign Ministers of Egypt, Syria and the six Gulf Co-operation Council (GCC) member states (Saudi Arabia, Kuwait, Bahrain, Qatar, the United Arab Emirates and Oman) issued the initial draft of their 'Damascus Declaration'. Never before had it been spelled out so clearly and publicly that peace in one part of the Middle East, namely the Gulf, was dependent on the resolution of conflicts elsewhere in the region, especially in the Arab–Israeli sector. Both Bush and the Arab members of the wartime coalition emphasized the need for region-wide co-operation in the pursuit of peace and prosperity. By contrast, the security arrangements that have actually taken shape have been mostly in the form of bilateral defence pacts and selective arms sales and training agreements, between the Western powers on the one hand and individual Middle Eastern states on the other.

While not totally defunct from an early stage, as some would claim, the Damascus Declaration has certainly not been realized in its entirety.

As a statement of political principles and economic aspirations it has constituted a fair reflection of the hopes of its signatories. As a framework for Gulf security arrangements, however, it quickly fell short of its original promise.

VISIONS OF A NEW ERA OF PEACE

The Gulf crisis, triggered by Iraq's invasion of Kuwait, took place in the context of a new, post-Cold War world, when optimism about the advent of a peaceful era in international relations was at its height. The crisis itself, and especially the ensuing war to retrieve Kuwait, consumed attention across the globe. Given that it attained such singular importance, and divided public opinion so deeply in the region itself, the whole event had the attributes of a watershed in the contemporary history of the Middle East. Perhaps because of this, when the war was over, the time seemed ripe for the victors to make a brand new beginning in a region beset with conflicts.

On the one side were those who fought in the coalition to free Kuwait and diminish the military capacity of Iraq; on the other side were those who opposed the resort to war. The divide was between those who sought to uphold the *status quo ante* the invasion of Kuwait, and those who questioned the justice of that *status quo* and, in the case of the Iraqi leader Saddam Hussein, were prepared to use force to change it. The military victory of the coalition over Iraq appeared to open the way for a peace-time alliance linking the GCC states, Egypt and Syria with the Western powers, and even (by extension) Turkey, a fellow member of the North Atlantic Treaty Organization (NATO). The prevailing mood and the substantially altered balance of power also seemed to pave the way for a resolution of the Arab–Israeli conflict. Meanwhile, a rapprochement between Iran and the GCC states was apparently in the making. Consequently, it was possible to envisage moving towards a new regional order, with co-operation on economic development, environmental protection, resource allocation and arms control.

President Bush's vision, as he expressed it to Congress on 6 March 1991, was based on the need to meet four main challenges.[1] First, he said, 'we must work together to create shared security arrangements in the region'. The primary responsibility for regional security would rest with the Middle Eastern states themselves, he believed, but America was ready to help:

This does not mean stationing US ground forces in the Arabian Peninsula, but it does mean American participation in joint exercises involving both air and ground forces. It means maintaining a capable US naval presence in the region just as we have for over 40 years. Let it be clear: our vital national interests depend on a stable and secure Gulf.

Secondly, according to the President, action would have to be taken to control the proliferation of weapons of mass destruction and the missiles used to deliver them, and Iraq in particular, 'must not have access to the instruments of war'. Thirdly, Bush maintained, the time had come to put an end to the Arab–Israeli conflict, in a comprehensive peace, 'grounded in UN Security Council Resolutions 242 and 338 and the principle of territory for peace'. Finally, the President called for an effort to foster economic freedom and prosperity for all the people of the region.

Broadly, the Damascus Declaration dovetailed with the US perspective. The GCC states, Egypt and Syria pledged their co-operation and co-ordination on the basis of five principles:

1. Working in accordance with the charters of the Arab League, the UN and other Arab and international charters, respecting and promoting the historical and fraternal ties and the relations of neighbourliness; commitment to respect the unity and territorial integrity, the equality of sovereignty, the inadmissibility of seizing territories by force, non-intervention in domestic affairs; and commitment to settling disputes by peaceful means.

2. To build a new Arab order to bolster joint Arab action. The arrangements agreed among the parties concerned shall be considered a basis for achieving this. The door will be left open before the other Arab states to contribute to this declaration in light of the agreement of interests and objectives.

3. To enable the Arab nation to direct all its resources to confronting the challenges threatening security and stability in the region, and to achieve a just and comprehensive solution to the Arab–Israeli conflict and the Palestine question based on the UN Charter and its pertinent resolutions.

4. To bolster economic co-operation among the parties concerned in order to establish an economic group among them with the objective of achieving economic and social development.

5. To respect the principle of each Arab state's sovereignty over its natural and economic resources.[2]

The Declaration also stated the hope that the Middle East could be declared a zone free of weapons of mass destruction, especially nuclear arms. More specifically, according to the first draft of the Declaration issued on 6 March 1991, the signatories anticipated that the Egyptian and Syrian troops remaining in the Gulf after the war, would represent 'a nucleus for an Arab peace force to be prepared so as to guarantee the security and safety of the Arab states in the Gulf region, and an example that would guarantee the effectiveness of the comprehensive Arab defence order'.[3]

The Egyptian forces in question consisted of one mechanized and one armoured division, together with some commando units, totalling 36,000 men and 400 tanks. The Syrian contribution, meanwhile, amounted to an armoured division and special forces brigade, totalling 19,000 men with 250 tanks.[4] Though not actually spelled out in Damascus, meanwhile, it was generally assumed that, in return for Egyptian and Syrian military assistance, the GCC states could be expected to provide financial assistance to Egypt and Syria, by investing in their development and awarding them business contracts.

Comparing the Damascus Declaration with President Bush's speech, it is evident that the two visions for Middle Eastern security had certain elements in common. Both envisaged more effective Arab defence co-operation, arms control, an Arab–Israeli peace and regional economic development. The US scenario did not stipulate which Arabs should co-operate for mutual defence, although Bush did talk about 'our friends and allies' taking primary responsibility for regional security. Meanwhile, the Damascus Declaration did not mention, and thus did not specifically rule out, a role for external powers in Arab defence plans.

Early assessments of how the new security framework for the Gulf would look discerned a three-tier arrangement, with the GCC forming the core, broader Arab support providing a more sizeable military alliance and, beyond that, an overarching or 'over-the-horizon' Western defence shield. In fact, the term preferred by Britain to describe the nature of Western assistance in Gulf defence was 'underpinning', which implied the kind of help to the GCC states that was bound to be required. The individual Gulf states turned to their Western allies for new supplies of arms and related maintenance and training agreements. Inevitably, therefore, the Western powers were to be closely involved at the core level of the security structure, as well as providing an 'over-the-horizon' deterrent.

REVISING THE TERMS OF THE DECLARATION

It was not long after the signing of the first draft of the Damascus Declaration that the GCC states began to show signs of having second thoughts about hosting a long-term Egyptian and Syrian military presence in the Gulf. Their thinking was influenced by various considerations. From a strategic point of view, there seemed little reason to recruit Egyptian and Syrian military backing if superior Western assistance was not only available but necessary, certainly in the event of a serious contingency. On the political front, meanwhile, Iran challenged the principle of an Arab alliance to protect the Gulf, including such far-removed powers as Egypt, but excluding Iran itself, even though it has the longest Gulf coast and has a fundamental and legitimate role in all issues pertaining to Gulf security. Friction between Tehran and Cairo, dating from the advent of the theocratic revolutionary government in Iran and Egypt's support for Iraq during the Iran–Iraq War, compounded Iran's hostility to Egyptian involvement in Gulf security.[5]

The GCC states also had economic reasons for wanting to backtrack on the expectations implicit in the original Damascus Declaration. They had war debts to settle, reconstruction costs to meet (especially in the case of Kuwait) and rearmament plans to implement. With these as their priorities and short-term cash-flow problems, they were not ready to lavish economic aid on Egypt and Syria in return for their continued provision of troops. In fact, the continuance of that military presence began to look like a liability.[6] The logic of defence co-operation dictated that such troops engage in joint exercises with their GCC partners. However, this could have compromised the supremacy of GCC military commanders in their own countries, and fraternization between the soldiers might have undermined established arrangements for controlling internal security in the Gulf states.

The extent of Egyptian disappointment with lack of progress on the military and financial provisions of the original Damascus agreement became apparent in May 1991. The bulk of lucrative contracts on offer in wartorn Kuwait had been granted to US companies, with British firms taking much of what remained – leaving little for Egyptian contractors. An expected boom in demand for Egyptian labourers and technicians in the Gulf, following the politically motivated dismissal of Palestinians, Jordanians, Yemenis and Sudanese, did not materialize. Such jobs as were available were most often given to Asian expatriates, apparently on the grounds that these were less likely to integrate with the host community and could thus be more readily controlled or dispensed with. True, the Gulf states had written off some of Egypt's debts, in recognition of the Egyptian contribution to the war effort, but from Cairo's perspective this seemed little more than an acknowledgement that such debts could never be redeemed anyway.[7] Meanwhile, all the GCC states, and Kuwait in particular, procrastinated on the issue of a joint Arab defence force for the Gulf.

On 8 May 1991 Egyptian President Hosni Mubarak announced that he was bringing Egypt's forces home from the Gulf, since they had completed their original mission.[8] That same day, US Defence Secretary Richard Cheney told Kuwait that Washington was prepared to retain a 5,000-man armoured brigade there for a while, after other US forces had withdrawn.[9] Britain made a similar statement with respect to its 1,000 or so troops in Kuwait. In other words, Kuwait chose the Western powers over fellow Arab countries to take care of even its short-term defence requirements, let alone its longer-term needs. In contrast to Egypt, Syria did not make public its views on the implementation of the Damascus Declaration. Arguably, Syria had more reason to value a reciprocal, if tacit, understanding with the Gulf states not to interfere in the security arrangements of others. Whilst Egypt risked losing further financial assistance by displaying pique, Syria may have calculated that it could extract a price for agreeing to leave the Gulf quietly.

As it was, Mubarak's announcement prompted Kuwait to deny any differences of opinion with Egypt.[10] There followed several weeks of bilateral contacts and consultations between the signatories of the Damascus Declaration. Commentary in the international press suggested that the parties were considering keeping a token Egyptian and Syrian troop presence in the Gulf for symbolic reasons, but on a much reduced scale. The reports referred to a draft plan for a joint Arab force totalling 26,000 troops to defend Kuwait, composed of 10,000 Saudis, 10,000 other GCC troops and 3,000 each from Egypt and Syria.

Meeting in Kuwait on 16 July 1991, the Foreign Ministers of the GCC states, Egypt and Syria approved a 'final' draft of the Damascus Declaration. In this there was no mention of Egyptian and Syrian forces forming the nucleus of an Arab peace force: instead, the agreement stated simply that, 'any GCC country has the right to employ the services of Egyptian and Syrian forces on its territories if it so wishes'.[11] On this basis, the signatories further declared their intention to seek to formulate a comprehensive protocol, adding to the mutual commitments existing among Arab countries, and to deposit that protocol with the Arab League. The protocol, they said, would represent a practical method to guarantee the security and safety of Arab countries and provide a blueprint for a comprehensive Arab defence and security system.

Another change to the wording of the original draft of the Declaration altered the fifth principle of co-ordination and co-operation, noted above, to read: 'To uphold the sovereignty of every Arab country and its control of its natural and economic resources'.

While the Arab victors of the 1991 Gulf War were thus engaged in defining their alliance, the leading Western members of the coalition were separately involved in dealing with post-Gulf War Iraq. Aside from liberating Kuwait, the allied air campaign had been intended to achieve the additional aim of demolishing Iraq's nuclear, biological and chemical (NBC) warfare capabilities and potential. The terms of the cease-fire, embodied in United Nations Security Council Resolution 687, were designed to complete this objective. Revelations of the extent of Iraq's arsenal and its efforts to conceal this only served to galvanize allied determination to disarm the country. The task was undertaken through the UN, with the US in the forefront.

From the moment when the advance of Operation Desert Storm was halted, it was hoped by the coalition partners that Saddam Hussein would not be able to survive in power long, after the humiliation of his defeat in Kuwait. Nonetheless, no assistance was given to the revolts which erupted in predominantly Shia-populated southern Iraq and across Iraqi Kurdistan to the north, for fear that the country could fragment and Iran would extend its influence. Allied hopes rested on the possibility of a *coup d'état* from within the Iraqi military. The fallout from Baghdad's counter-offensive against the Kurds, with thousands of refugees fleeing to the northern borders with Turkey and Iran, nonetheless did oblige the Western allies to act. The operation to rescue and escort the Kurds back into northern Iraq defused a much publicized humanitarian disaster and protected Turkey from an unwanted and destabilizing influx of Kurdish refugees. Thereafter, the Kurds were given allied air protection north of the 36th parallel, while Turkish forces established a *cordon sanitaire* along the border between Iraq and Kurdish-populated south-east Turkey, itself in the throes of a battle between Kurdish separatists and the security forces.

EACH TO ITS OWN

Among the members of the GCC, it is Kuwait which has been most eager to secure Western commitment to its defence in the future. The Iraqi invasion demonstrated just how vulnerable the Emirate is and how reliant upon others it must be for protection. The experiences of 1990–91 were obviously scarring for the Kuwaitis and seemingly left them with few illusions about the realities of power and the limits of what wealth can buy. Not trusting to professions of brotherly love from anyone, they made little apology for acquiring the best military assistance available.

On 24 August 1991 the Deputy Speaker of the Kuwait National Council announced that the terms for a ten-year defence agreement with the US had been finalized. Commenting later on those terms, Kuwaiti Defence Minister Ali Sabah al-Salim denied that the pact was in any sense a 'protection' agreement, saying it was concerned with military co-operation to keep the peace in the region, the protection of the two countries, the storage of weapons and military equipment, and the carrying out of joint manoeuvres in Kuwait on land, at sea and in the air. The Minister added that he did not support the idea of the presence of foreign bases in Kuwait, 'because Kuwait is small and the presence of bases makes it threatened all the time because of its proximity to the enemy'.[12] He also noted that the Gulf armies would not deter any possible Iraqi attack because they were represented symbolically in Kuwait and did not have the capability for rapid deployment possessed by the superpowers. Reports circulating at the time suggested that it was the US, not Kuwait, which had resisted the idea of foreign bases actually in the Emirate, in preference for an off-shore naval presence and rapid deployment in time of need.[13]

The US–Kuwait defence agreement was formally signed in Washington by Richard Cheney and Ali Sabah al-Salim on 19 September 1991. Commentary indicated that Kuwait was likely to contribute some $10 million for the maintenance and warehousing of prepositioned equipment sufficient for three armoured companies and three mechanized companies of US forces, as well as building a new military base in southern Kuwait and providing around $35 million annually for joint training exercises and acquiring new arms for the Kuwaiti forces.[14] The agreement obviated the need for the presence of the US troops whose stay in Kuwait had been extended the previous May. In November 1991 a series of joint military exercises began. Their frequency, together with the assignment of a US military training contingent to the Kuwaiti armed forces, in fact amounted to a continuous US presence in the Emirate following the expulsion of the Iraqi army.

At the same time as reaching agreement with the US, Kuwait indicated that it intended to sign additional pacts with Britain and France. On 11 February 1992 a memorandum on security co-operation was signed by the British and Kuwaiti Defence Ministers in London. The text was not made public, but reports indicated that the British agreed to consult and co-operate with the Kuwaiti armed forces in their efforts to defend the territory and sovereignty of the Emirate. The setting up of a defence committee was anticipated, along with provision of training and equipment by Britain, though there were no plans to preposition British military supplies.[15] Subsequently, on 18 August 1992, the Kuwaiti Defence Minister signed another ten-year defence agreement, this time with his French counterpart in Paris. As with the US and Anglo-Kuwaiti pacts, provision was made for military co-operation, the drawing up of training programmes and the exchange of expertise, but no permanent stationing of foreign forces in the Emirate. However, in this instance, according to Sheikh Ali Sabah al-Salim, the agreement guaranteed the direct defence of Kuwait on the part of France, without any prior consultation between the two countries, in the event of Kuwait being subjected to an external threat.[16]

Among the members of the GCC, Kuwait stands out as a special case not only because it is directly overshadowed and endangered by Iraq, but also because, after achieving full independence from Britain in 1961, the Emirate had chosen a few years later to end its 1961 agreement with the United Kingdom, providing for British assistance on request, and had tried to steer a course of non-alignment thereafter. By contrast, Britain's other former 'protected states', Bahrain, Qatar and the United Arab Emirates (the UAE, formerly known as the Trucial States), retained Treaties of Friendship with the UK following their independence in 1971. According to these Treaties, the contracting parties, 'conscious of their common interest in the peace and stability of the region', have agreed to 'consult together on matters of mutual concern in time of need'.[17]

Whether the maintenance of such an agreement with Britain by Kuwait could have saved the Emirate from the Iraqi invasion is doubtful. Admittedly, Britain had deployed forces there in 1961, just after Kuwait became independent, to deter an Iraqi invasion threat. However, at that point Britain was still acting as military guarantor of Gulf security. Nonetheless, after the experience of an actual Iraqi invasion, Kuwait was taking no more chances, and signed up for military assistance with the US, Britain and France. Furthermore, Kuwait also announced its intention to establish a defence agreement with Russia.[18] To draw attention to the significance of Kuwait's policy reversal, when the details of its security pact with the US became known, the Iraqi government called on the Non-Aligned Movement to expel Kuwait from its membership. However, the extent of Kuwait's predicament was all too apparent when, on the anniversary of Iraq's invasion of Kuwait, at the beginning of August 1992, Saddam Hussein's government repeated its claim to the Emirate.

Meanwhile, Bahrain, Qatar and the UAE have sought to increase their ties to the Western powers, for fear of losing their independence. Unlike its richer allies in the GCC, Bahrain cannot afford to pay for US supplies and support. As a result, Bahrain has secured new American aid and training to enhance its armed forces, through an agreement signed on 22 October 1991, which, under the rubric of defence cooperation, will presumably allow the US to make some use of Bahrain as a strategic facility for the purposes of its own naval and related air and intelligence-gathering activities in the Gulf. Qatar, which faces little difficulty with defence budgeting, signed a defence pact with the US on 23 June 1992 and has been courted by France for defence sales agreements. The UAE finalized a framework agreement with France on 10 September 1991, allowing for joint manoeuvres and experiments on the French Leclerc tank.[19] The Emirates have also discussed terms for an understanding with the US.

For Oman the situation is somewhat different. Its historical relationship with Britain had preserved the formal independence of the Sultanate, while allowing for British assistance in defence and security. An Exchange of Letters Concerning the Sultan's Armed Forces, Civil Aviation, RAF Facilities and Economic Development, dated 25 July 1958, has remained the basis for UK–Omani relations.[20] However, Britain's involvement in Omani defence has much diminished and technical arrangements, such as the assignment of British Loan Service personnel and the employment of British contract officers, have been renegotiated over time, as in the wake of the 1991 Gulf War. US treaty relations with Oman also date from the 1950s, though again the administrative details have been changed over time and a secret agreement was negotiated on the use of facilities on Masirah Island. For the Sultanate, therefore, the 1991 Gulf War did not represent a significant new point of departure in its relations with the Western powers.

Alone among the GCC states, Saudi Arabia has held back from defining the exact parameters of its military ties to the West following the Desert Storm campaign. The Kingdom has agreed to a series of arms purchases and training packages with the US, Britain and France over the past 40 years, but these provide for the administration of such deals, not the nature of defence commitments in time of need. As will be seen, the reasons for Saudi reticence about outlining more detailed arrangements for the future have to do with domestic politics in the Kingdom as well as its relations with other members of the GCC. In common with these, however, Riyadh has put liaison with the Western powers ahead of implementation of the Damascus Declaration.

Lack of progress on this and, in particular, Kuwait's obvious preference for cementing bilateral pacts with outside powers first, has given rise to much comment and some criticism in the Arab press. At the announcement of the US–Kuwaiti agreement, the Kuwaiti Minister of Defence said there was no contradiction between this and the Damascus Declaration: the two, he claimed, were complementary. Egypt's Foreign Minister, meanwhile, signalled 'respect for Kuwait's entitlement to protect its own interests' and described the Damascus Declaration as independent of any other arrangements because it aimed to achieve unified, inter-Arab security and was based on specifically Arab considerations and charters.[21] As indicated by these comments, however, the Egyptians and, as it emerged, the Syrians too, were sensitive about being written out of Gulf security entirely.

A meeting of representatives from the six GCC states, Egypt and Syria (the so-called 'six-plus-two') in Cairo during November 1991 gave rise to reports that the idea of stationing Syrian and Egyptian contingents in the Gulf had been shelved in favour of a scheme for an Arab rapid deployment force. Objections from Iran were cited as an explanation for the change of heart. A separate meeting of the GCC states alone, in December, fell short of its objective of devising a formula for an integrated GCC force. At the beginning of March 1992, Egypt sought an explanation from the British Foreign Office about Foreign Minister Douglas Hogg's comments to the effect that Egypt and Syria were not involved in the security of the Gulf region, since they do not overlook it, whereas Iran's role could not be ignored.[22] The Syrian press raised similar concerns about Hogg's remarks, saying that Gulf security is first and last an Arab responsibility and, according to the newspaper *Tishrin*: 'Syria will respond to appeals by any brother who might ask for help and assistance without any consideration for the oil and material interests which govern the West's behaviour and conduct'.[23]

Also in March 1992, there were other indications that the Gulf War coalition had broken ranks, when both Egypt and Syria let it be known that they were opposed to any further use of force against Iraq, in support of UN resolutions, even as the US and its Western allies were hinting that such force might be employed.

In late April, pending an expected meeting of the Damascus Declaration signatory countries in May, the Egyptian Foreign Minister and, unusually, Syrian President Hafiz al-Asad toured the Gulf states. According to the Egyptian Minister Amr Musa, the tour was very useful in terms of co-ordination and reviewing current stands and problems in the Arab world, particularly the Gulf, and that views were exchanged frankly and objectively.[24] A report in Cairo's *Misr al-Fatah*, however, asserted that Musa had been told by the Gulf states that they were agreed among themselves on a new security formula, 'which is a purely internal GCC matter and does not concern Egypt or Syria'.[25] The paper also claimed that strong differences had emerged over the interpretation of the Damascus Declaration and the GCC states were intending to conclude security agreements with each of Iran, Egypt and Syria separately. Attempts were made by the Gulf states to deny any problems with the Declaration, but they subsequently decided on a postponement of the 'six-plus-two' meeting scheduled for the end of May.

PROBLEMS FACING THE GCC

The problem with implementing the Damascus Declaration was not merely that the individual members of the GCC showed a preference for bilateral agreements with the Western powers. Both the Western and the Arab visions for Gulf security, as outlined on 6 March 1991, were stymied by the inability of the core GCC states to agree among themselves on a co-ordinated approach. Their difficulties stemmed from two factors: first, the need to address unpalatable decisions about the nature, structure and purpose of their individual defence establishments; and secondly, lack of trust towards each other. Not until they had worked out the first issue could the GCC states tackle the second, yet the two could not be dealt with in total isolation, or without regard to the prospects and shape of Western defence commitments.

As a unified whole the GCC alliance makes some military sense, but on their own the smaller states especially cannot hope to stand up to more powerful neighbours. After the liberation from Iraq, the total number of Kuwaiti citizens considered as true Kuwaitis is approximately 610,000. Whereas before the invasion the Emirate's armed forces numbered upwards of 20,000 men, by December 1991 they could claim an enrolment of only about 7,000–10,000.[26] Bahrain's population, estimated at nearly 500,000, of which about 60 per cent could be categorized as Bahrainis, had some 9,500 in the armed forces. Qatar, with an estimated population of 420,000, a quarter of them Qatari, had 8,000 men under arms. The UAE, whose population numbered 1.5 million, including about 285,000 UAE nationals, had a total of 48,000 men in its forces. Oman's population was also about 1.5 million, though there the majority are Omani nationals and in late 1991 the armed forces totalled 27,000 regulars and several thousand more in paramilitary units. Meanwhile, in Saudi Arabia, with an indigenous population of upwards of 8 million, the combined strength of the armed forces and the National Guard was about 120,000 men.[27]

The geographical contrasts between these states are obvious, with the Bahrain islands encompassing 676 square kilometres at one end of the scale and Saudi Arabia encompassing about 2,331,000 square kilometres (depending on how the borders are defined) at the other end of the spectrum. Whereas the Saudi defence budget in 1990 was $13.8 billion, that of Bahrain, the poorest of the GCC states, was estimated at $193.9 million.[28] In the oil boom years of the 1970s and early 1980s, the newly independent small states set about acquiring equipment for land, air and naval forces, while the Saudis and Omanis expanded their arsenals. However, they did not follow a co-ordinated policy in their acquisitions, even after the formation of the GCC in 1981. Separate security concerns, not least the suspicions of the smaller states about the ambitions of their larger allies, prevented the GCC members from sharing information and combining their strength, except at a token level.

The Gulf War has not removed these obstacles to integration. The dispute between Qatar and Bahrain over possession of the Hawar Islands and surrounding waters has resurfaced, and the borders between Qatar, the UAE and Oman on the one hand and between each of these and Saudi Arabia on the other, have yet to be finalized. Resort to war over these border issues could not be considered likely, in the post-Gulf War setting, but agreement on a joint force has proved elusive. At their summit meeting in December 1991 the GCC leaders reportedly discussed schemes such as an Omani suggestion for a combined force of about 100,000, with the Sultanate providing much of the manpower and the smaller, oil-rich states making their contributions more in terms of money. Finding a formula for where to base the forces, and under whose command, apparently proved too problematic for a final decision to be reached.

In his address to the December 1991 GCC summit, King Fahd of Saudi Arabia rejected the use or threat of force to achieve expansionist aims and economic ambitions, and said:

> It is only natural that our experience should influence matters in the region and be an incentive for a future single outlook. It is no longer acceptable to allow our region's security to be the target of those who have ambitions for expansion and domination. Therefore our interest at the current stage has been devoted to the future security arrangements. In this we proceed from a view which depends on self-reliance and co-operation with the friendly states in everything that serves the aims of security and stability in our region.[29]

The final statement issued at the close of the summit echoed the same general sentiments and, without defining any specifics, said:

> Proceeding from its firm conviction of the importance of strengthening security and military co-operation between the member states, and the reinforcing of their defence capabilities in the light of the lessons drawn from the aggression of the Iraqi regime, the higher council affirmed its determination to continue co-ordination and co-operation in the military and security fields, and to promote defence capabilities in the framework of a unified strategic concept that meets the requirements of security, faces up to the challenges of the situation, realizes stability and guarantees the non-recurrence of such an aggression.[30]

The statement also said the Council looked forward to realization of the principles and objectives of the Damascus Declaration and affirmed its, 'eagerness to give momentum to bilateral relations with the Islamic Republic of Iran'.

In sum, therefore, the GCC demurred on fixing the specific details of an integrated security structure among the member states, thereby also leaving unrealized the defence component of the Damascus Declaration. Meanwhile, the smaller states, with Kuwait at the forefront, went

ahead with defining their individual defence agreements with the Western powers.

The reasons for Saudi Arabia's reticence on this score are multiple.
As the 1990–91 Gulf conflict demonstrated, Saudi Arabia faces a potential threat from Iraq, and possibly others, which it is unable to
counter by itself. Also, the Kingdom is not in a position to defend
smaller allies, such as Kuwait, from the same dangers, without external
assistance. However, even assuming that help is forthcoming in the
event of an emergency, it takes time and money to deploy foreign
forces to the Gulf. Logically, therefore, it would make sense to at least
preposition equipment as a precaution. This Kuwait has agreed to do.
However, Kuwait is too small and too vulnerable to provide safe and
strategically useful facilities for a major engagement such as Desert
Shield or Desert Storm. Bahrain, even if willing, is also too small and
vulnerable, and Oman is too far away from the potential danger zone.
Thus the protection of any member of the GCC from an external threat
critically depends on the co-operation of Saudi Arabia, with its formidable strategic depth and frontage on the Red Sea as well as the Gulf.

The issue of prepositioning proved to be one of the first stumbling
blocks in Saudi negotiations with the US following the liberation of
Kuwait.[31] Not surprisingly, the US would insist on protecting its own
prepositioned equipment with its own personnel, but the scale of the
requirement would be such that there might be little to distinguish
between facilities for prepositioning and an American base, or bases,
on Saudi soil. That prospect being politically unacceptable, the Saudis
apparently procrastinated. Pending a decision, however, some supplies
left behind by the US forces after the Gulf War have remained in place.

Another requirement for Western commitment to Saudi, and broader
GCC, defence, is that the indigenous forces be better prepared than
they were in 1990 to receive, assist and co-ordinate with foreign forces
arriving on rapid deployment. The Saudis themselves have plenty of
incentives for wanting to improve the preparedness, organization and
capabilities of their military establishment. During the Gulf crisis the
Saudi authorities were criticized by their own citizens for seemingly
having so little to show for their massive defence expenditures over
preceding years. In the wake of the war, the government and its critics
share an interest in reducing Saudi reliance on external protectors.

Expanding the Saudi armed forces nonetheless presents the government with some virtually insuperable political problems. Immediately
after the end of the 1991 Gulf War there was talk of tripling the size of

the Saudi military which, as noted, numbers upwards of 100,000, counting the National Guard and tribal levies.[32] The latter two components make up the majority of the whole, and the National Guard is specifically tasked with security within the borders of the Kingdom, especially security for the Hajj, and therefore cannot, under its present brief, deploy beyond those borders. Saudi practice has been to select those serving in the forces on the basis of regional origin, tribal affiliations and traditions of loyalty to the regime. Consequently, the Saudi Shia community, concentrated in the east, and the Hijazis of the west are under-represented.

To expand significantly the Saudi forces would require either the introduction of universal conscription and ending selective recruitment, or else filling the ranks with foreigners, such as Pakistanis. Neither option is attractive and the latter is contradictory to the aim of enhancing the Kingdom's indigenous defence capabilities. The native Saudi population (8 million, or more, according to official statistics) is growing rapidly and is expected to double over the next 15 years, presenting the need to create new sources of employment. There is, therefore, a pool of potential new recruits over the longer term, but even so the Saudi population is outnumbered by that of Yemen (10 million) and dwarfed by those of Iraq (18 million) and especially Iran (60 million). All the Saudis can hope for, therefore, is a somewhat expanded, more efficient and better trained military equipped with the best technology that money can buy.

Realizing this aspiration, nonetheless, inevitably entails reliance on Western allies to provide the necessary equipment and training, and presupposes sustaining a sizeable defence budget. In other words, the Saudis are caught in a dilemma, with little alternative but to continue their reliance on foreigners for key aspects of their defence arrangements. Since the end of the 1991 Gulf War they have been invited by Western contractors to buy more high technology defence systems. Competition has been hot, given that the fate of production lines and jobs at firms like McDonnell Douglas in the US and British Aerospace in the UK rests on their export orders. The leverage works both ways, of course, and the Saudis are fully aware of their capacity to bind Western contractors, and hence governments, into their defence arrangements.

This does not alter the fact, however, that the Saudi rulers must maintain the support of their own population for heavy defence budgets and the concomitant involvement of foreigners in defence planning.

Consequently, the post-Gulf War priority for the Saudi leadership has been political rather than military. Decisions on the latter were deferred, except for placing an order with the US for 72 F-15s, ahead of the US elections of 3 November 1992. While Congressional approval for this sale was forthcoming, the terms of the deal have been subject to lengthy negotiations. Meanwhile, the Saudis put on hold plans to build a new air base at Al Sulayyil, in the heart of the Arabian Peninsula, and delayed for a while their decision to buy more British Tornados, while the government in Riyadh drew up plans for regional and national political changes.

On 1 March 1992, King Fahd announced the inauguration of a new 'basic statute of governing', a statute on regional organization and a statute establishing a consultative council, or Majlis al-Shura. The package amounted to a formal constitution for the Saudi Kingdom, based on Islamic law, or *Sharia*, but also providing rules on the protection of personal freedoms, including protections from arbitrary arrest and search.[33] The King also made arrangements for a form of electoral college, composed of 500 princes, to decide the succession to the throne and thereby involve more and younger members of the royal family in selecting the monarch. The powers of the Majlis al-Shura do not extend to overriding the King's authority and, since the members have all been appointed rather than elected, some of the more progressive elements in the Kingdom, whether Islamicists or secularists, have been less than satisfied.[34]

POST-GULF WAR SECURITY PUT TO THE TEST

Having delayed a meeting originally planned for May 1992, the signatories of the Damascus Declaration eventually convened in Doha on 9 September 1992. By that time, two separate crises, involving Iraq on the one hand and Iran on the other, had presented new challenges to Gulf security.

In July the Baghdad government denied UN weapons inspectors access to the Iraqi Ministry of Agriculture on the grounds that their mandate to strip Iraq of its NBC capability did not entitle them to enter government premises not directly involved in munitions procurement. After a stand-off of several days a new UN team, not including US personnel, was finally allowed access under a compromise arrangement. No weapons-related materials were found and Iraq appeared to have won a political victory. The incident gave rise to threats from the US that force might again be used against Iraq if it continued to obstruct UN operations, and on 26 August the US, Britain and France announced the imposition of a 'no-fly zone' south of the 32nd parallel in Iraq.

This new move was described as an open-ended commitment to protect the Shia population of southern Iraq from repression at the hands of the Iraqi regime and, according to a US Pentagon spokesman: 'If Iraq violates the "no-fly" rule, the coalition forces will respond appropriately and decisively', though he would not specify the precise rules of engagement.[35] To implement their decision, the US and Britain began aerial patrols of southern Iraq from the Dhahran air base in Saudi Arabia and from US aircraft carriers in the Gulf. However, the initial impact proved somewhat of an anticlimax, since the Iraqi airforce declined to challenge the 'air-exclusion zone', while reports persisted of continuing clashes on the ground between forces loyal to Saddam and rebel elements.

With the benefit of hindsight it was apparent that the allied decision to police southern Iraqi airspace had been reached only after an earlier plan to launch attacks on Iraqi military installations, in reprisal for Baghdad's challenge to UN weapons inspectors, had to be aborted following leaks to the press.[36] To have gone ahead with the initial scheme would have been to invite condemnation for blatant manipulation of foreign policy for electioneering purposes by President Bush. As it was, the Arab press revealed widespread unease about the possibility of renewed military action against Iraq, when that country had already 'suffered enough' in the eyes of many Arabs, and while Israel's Arab enemies were being encouraged to make peace with the Jewish state, despite the latter's reluctance over the years to implement to the letter UN resolutions regarding the Palestinians and the occupied territories.

The Arab states were also unhappy about the possible repercussions of the imposition of the 'no-fly zone'. Much of Iraqi Kurdistan, where the Western allies had implemented their 'safe-haven' policy, was already insulated from the authority of Baghdad and now, it seemed, the predominantly Shia south was to be encouraged to secede as well, suggesting the fragmentation or partition of Iraq. Whether or not this could come to pass, Sunni Arabs saw a danger of Iran increasing its influence over the Iraqi Shia through infiltration, under the protection of the 'no-fly zone'. There was concern, too, that the Western allies were setting a dangerous precedent for interference in the internal affairs of a sovereign state.

For a variety of reasons, therefore, the GCC states proved less than enthusiastic about assisting their Western allies in implementation of their policy towards Iraq. Their reticence led to delays in deploying allied air forces to the Gulf in August 1992 for the new Operation Southern Watch.[37] Notwithstanding Britain's Treaty of Friendship with Bahrain, the UK's contribution to the 1991 Gulf War effort and an Anglo-Bahraini military co-operation agreement, signed on 28 July 1992,[38] British Tornados deployed to the Gulf to police the 'no-fly zone' were refused permission to operate from Bahrain. In the end, the US apparently prevailed on the Saudis to allow the Western allies to operate from Dhahran, but with minimal co-operation from the Kingdom and no provision of headquarters facilities inside the Saudi Ministry of Defence. The reluctance of the GCC states to co-ordinate with their Western allies in their continuing confrontation with Iraq, pointed to the weaknesses in the relationships designed to 'underpin' Gulf security in the wake of the 1991 Gulf War.[39] Meanwhile, a dispute between Iran and the UAE over Abu Musa and the Greater and Lesser Tunbs islands in the Gulf served as a reminder that Iraq was not the only potential threat to the security of the GCC states.

Under the terms of an agreement reached between Iran and the Emirate of Sharjah in 1971, when Britain withdrew from the Gulf and Iran challenged Sharjah over ownership of Abu Musa, this island had been administered jointly by Iran and the Emirate. In April 1992, however, Iran refused entry to foreign workers hired by Sharjah to work on Abu Musa and was reported to be denying residence on the island to all those without permits approved by Tehran. Mediation by Oman failed to resolve the issue and it resurfaced in August 1992 when the government of the UAE accused Iran of turning away over one hundred of the island's residents, who had arrived on board a ship from Sharjah, on the grounds that they did not have the requisite permits. Whilst Iran claimed the right to vet entry to the island, Sharjah, with GCC backing, deemed this an infringement of its sovereign rights. As the dispute escalated, the UAE raised again the issue of Iranian occupation of the Tunbs as well as Abu Musa, while Iran questioned the grounds on which the UAE based its claims to sovereignty and accused outside powers of exploiting the dispute to harm relations between Iran and its Arab neighbours and to justify the foreign presence in the Gulf. The Abu Musa affair raised a number of questions about Gulf security.

It revived Arab and Western concerns about the ultimate ambitions of Iran: the very same concerns that had led many in both camps to support Iraq during its eight-year war with the Islamic Republic. By the same token, it showed how problematic is the situation of the GCC states, caught between wanting to avert crises with Iran by fostering better relations and wanting to bolster their defences against a potential Iranian threat. The affair also pointed to the inadequacies of reliance on Western protection, since this could serve as an irritant to peaceful relations between states in the region as well as an insurance against defeat in war. In a sense, however, the dispute over Abu Musa offered an opportunity for the Damascus Declaration to prove its worth. After all, Syria is not only a signatory to that pact but also a long-time friend of Iran within the Arab camp. As such Syria could be a valuable mediator in the affair and did apparently seek to perform this role.[40]

The political value of the Damascus Declaration was affirmed at the meeting of the signatories in Doha in September 1992. On the issue of military co-operation, however, the parties remained reticent, with Egypt apparently proposing the addition of several protocols covering economic and military co-operation, including the establishment of a joint rapid deployment force, while the GCC states still preferred to emphasize the political principles embodied in the Declaration.[41] Egypt's proposals envisaged that each of the eight states would keep on call 'a reasonable number' of trained troops which could be deployed quickly if any of the member states were threatened.[42] At the close of the Doha meeting, on 11 September, the Egyptian Foreign Minister, Amr Musa, said agreement had been reached to begin practical measures to implement the Damascus Declaration's military, political, economic, cultural and information clauses, but nothing was to be made public as yet.[43]

In the closing statement issued at the conclusion of the meeting in Qatar, on 11 September, the Damascus Declaration states affirmed the need for joint Arab action, as the 'safest way to protect the interests and destiny' of the Arab nation. They also referred to the commitment of the members of the Arab League to joint Arab defence and co-operation.[44] They were not, however, forthcoming on specifics. In addition, they affirmed their desire for a peaceful resolution of the Arab–Israeli conflict and the Palestine question, on the basis of Security Council Resolutions 242 and 338; urged Israel to comply with the nuclear non-proliferation treaty and proposals for a chemical weapons non-proliferation treaty; voiced concern at Iraq's continued non-compliance with UN resolutions and:

...reiterated their deep concern about Iraq's territorial integrity and its regional security, and held the Iraqi regime fully responsible for the suffering of the Iraqi people which results from the regime's refusal to implement UN Security Council Resolutions 706 and 712. They also praised the world community's concern about ending the annihilation campaigns waged by the Iraqi regime against the Iraqi people, and held the regime fully responsible for the consequences.[45]

In other words, the Damascus Declaration states welcomed international concern about the fate of the Iraqi people, while not actually endorsing the methods, such as the 'no-fly zone', purportedly adopted to protect those people. Meanwhile, they resorted to the familiar refrain of blaming Saddam Hussein for all that befell Iraq.

The September statement also tackled the issue of Abu Musa and the Tunbs, in notably unequivocal terms. Denouncing Iran's unjustified measures and encroachment on UAE territory, the Ministers called on Iran to honour the memorandum of understanding between Sharjah and Iran, 'affirming that Abu Musa island became the responsibility of the UAE government when the federation was established'. The Ministers also categorically rejected Iran's occupation of the Tunbs which, they said, also belonged to the UAE. There was not, however, a call for any specific action on the Arab side, merely a reiteration of the need for peaceful resolution of disputes.

On the subject of economic co-operation, meanwhile, the eight Ministers, 'recommended the formation of a committee bringing together their states' finance and economic ministers', to be co-ordinated by Qatar, and to present recommendations to the governments of the Damascus Declaration states. This provision was no more remarkable than the other issues dealt with in the document. All in all, the Damascus Declaration states displayed no more vigour about reaching decisions than had the GCC at *its* periodic summits. On the issue of military co-operation, in any case, it was unlikely that the 'six-plus-two' could succeed where the GCC had failed to make tangible progress.

CONCLUSION

The high point of co-operation between the GCC states, Egypt and Syria occurred in the 1991 Gulf War, prior to the formulation of the Damascus Declaration. As originally conceived, the 'six-plus-two' pact was designed to turn that wartime co-operation into a more permanent arrangement. However, the purpose behind the wartime alliance, namely the liberation of Kuwait, had been achieved. Meanwhile, Iraq as a threat had been much diminished and Iran began again to pose a more serious challenge to the Arab Gulf states. Any framework for Gulf security which excludes both Iraq and Iran has the appearance of an alliance against one or both of these Gulf powers, which may provoke more problems than it solves. Certainly, the various signatories of the Damascus Declaration have proved divided on how best to deal with Iran and how seriously to view the potential threat from Iraq.

In this context, the Damascus Declaration never had much prospect of succeeding as a military alliance. There are other problems, too. Unless and until the GCC can agree on an integrated defence structure, it seems unlikely that the 'six-plus-two' could do so either. Meanwhile, the existence of separate defence pacts between Gulf states and the Western powers, and the presence of Western forces in the area, undermines the impetus for an indigenous security structure and aggravates some of the existing tensions between the various countries in the region.

Whatever its military shortcomings, however, the Damascus Declaration has given expression to an important, if transitory, political alignment. Unlike the Arab League, which is too large and unwieldy to act decisively, the 'six-plus-two' did make some sense as a manageable alliance. The signatories shared a fundamental interest in their declared commitment to upholding the sovereignty of existing states, within their prevailing borders. Perhaps the real value of the Declaration, though, has derived from the framework it has provided for bilateral contacts between the signatories. It is little more than the sum of its parts, but for a while, at least, those parts have had reason to want to co-operate. This being so, it was only to be expected, perhaps, that the relevance and cohesion of the Damascus Declaration alignment would wane as new shifts took place in the regional power balance.

NOTES

1. President Bush, 'The World After the Persian Gulf War', address before a joint session of Congress, Washington, D.C., 6 March 1991, *US Department of State Despatch*, 11 March 1991, pp.161–3.
2. Text, as broadcast, of the 'Damascus Declaration', *Syrian Arab Republic Radio*, 6 March 1991, *BBC Summary of World Broadcasts (SWB)*, ME/1015, 8 March 1991, pp. A/9–10.

3. *Ibid.*
4. Other Arab forces committed to 'Desert Storm' included: Saudi Arabia 40,000 ground troops, 500 tanks and 180 tactical aircraft; Free Kuwait 7,000 troops, 60 tanks and 20 aircraft; other GCC 8,000 men, 24 tanks and 80 aircraft. 'War in the Gulf: Sovereignty, Oil and Security', Edward Foster and Rosemary Hollis, *RUSI Whitehall Paper*, No. 8 (1991).
5. 'Iranian Papers Comment on Damascus Declaration', *IRNA*, 7 March 1991, *SWB* ME/1016, 9 March 1991, p. A/14; 'Egyptian Response to Iranian Minister's Remarks about Gulf Security', *MENA*, 26 June 1991, *SWB* ME/1111, 29 June 1991, p. A/6.
6. 'Gulf Blueprint: Arabs Have 2nd Thoughts', *International Herald Tribune*, 18 May 1991; T. Walker, 'Gulf Security Issue Divides Arab Brothers', *Financial Times*, 30 May 1991.
7. Interviews conducted by the author in Cairo, May 1991.
8. Hedayat Abdel-Nabi, 'Egypt to Withdraw Forces from Gulf', *Al-Ahram Weekly*, 9 May 1991, p. 1.
9. 'Cheney Says US Will Keep Weapons in Gulf for Allies', *International Herald Tribune*, 10 May 1991; T. Walker, 'Gulf Security Issue Divides Arab Brothers', *Financial Times*, 30 May 1991.
10. 'Kuwaiti Foreign Minister Denies "Differences" Are Behind Egypt's Troop Pullout', *KUNA*, 11 May 1991, *SWB* ME/1070, 13 May 1991, p. A/12.
11. 'Final' Text of Damascus Declaration, *MENA* 6 August 1991, *SWB* ME/1145, 8 August 1991, pp. A/4–6.
12. 'Kuwaiti Minister on Protection Treaty with USA', *KUNA*, 31 August 1991, *SWB* ME/1166, 2 September 1991, pp. A/2–3.
13. B. Gellman, 'First Strand in Gulf Security Network', *International Herald Tribune*, 19 September 1991; 'Kuwait and US Defence Deal Agreed', *Independent*, 20 September 1991.
14. '"Backup Role" for the West', *Financial Times Survey on Kuwait*, 26 February 1992, p. iv.
15. 'Kuwaiti Defence Minister in UK to Sign Security and Defence Memorandum', *SWB* ME/1301, 11 February 1992, p. i; D. White, 'Kuwait Defence Pact Lifts UK Hopes of Sales', *Financial Times*, 12 February 1992.
16. 'Kuwait's Defence Agreement with France', *KUNA*, 18 August 1992, *SWB* ME/1464, 20 August 1992, p. A/15.
17. Treaty Series No. 79 (1971), Cmnd. 4828; Treaty Series No. 4 (1972), Cmnd. 4850; Treaty Series No. 35 (1972), Cmnd. 4937.
18. 'Russian Foreign Minister Visits Kuwait; Security Cooperation Treaty Discussed', *SWB* ME/1367, 29 April 1992, p. A/8.
19. 'UAE: Military Agreement Signed with France', *SWB* ME/1175, 12 September 1991, p. A/6.
20. Treaty Series No. 28 (1958) Cmnd. 507, as confirmed by D. Hurd in the House of Commons on 11 May 1983.
21. 'Egyptian and Kuwaiti Foreign Ministers Comment on Kuwaiti–US Protection Treaty', *Arab Republic of Egypt Radio*, 3 September 1991, *SWB* ME/1170, 6 September 1991, p. A/1.
22. 'Egyptian Government Seeks FCO Explanation of Hogg's Comments on Gulf Security', *Radio Monte Carlo*, 4 March 1992, *SWB* ME/1322, 6 March 1992, p. A/15.
23. 'Syrian Government Paper Rejects D. Hogg's Statement on Gulf Security', *Radio Monte Carlo*, 5 March 1992, *SWB* ME/1323, 7 March 1992, p. A/14.
24. 'Egyptian Foreign Minister Comments on His Gulf Tour', *MENA*, 26 April 1992, *SWB* ME/1367, 29 April 1992, p. A/5.

25. 'GCC Suggests "Freeze" on Damascus Declaration', *Misr Al-Fatah*, 27 April 1992, *US Foreign Broadcast Information Service* (*FBIS*) FBIS-NES-92-086, 4 May 1992, p. 5.
26. S. Gazit and Z. Eytan (1992), *The Middle East Military Balance 1990–91*, Tel Aviv University, Jaffee Centre for Strategic Studies: Jerusalem Post Press.
27. *Ibid.*
28. *Ibid.*
29. 'King Fahd's Address to the GCC Summit', *SPA*, 24 December 1991, *SWB* ME/ 1264, 28 December 1991, p. A/4.
30. 'Final Statement of the GCC Summit', *KUNA*, 25 December 1991, *SWB* ME/ 1264, 28 December 1991, p. A/5.
31. J. Miller, 'Big GI Presence? Saudis Balk', *International Herald Tribune*, 30 April 1991; B. Starr, 'Saudi Rejects US Basing Move', *Janes Defence Weekly*, 4 April 1992, p. 549.
32. D. Ottaway, 'Saudis May Triple Army Size', *International Herald Tribune*, 22 April 1991.
33. M. Nicholson, 'Saudi King to Set Up Consultative Council', *Financial Times*, 2 March 1992; 'Saudi Arabia: Basic Statutes', *SWB* ME/1319, 3 March 1992, pp. A/ 1-8.
34. 'Saudi Arabia: Chairman of Consultative Council Appointed', *SWB* ME/1489, 18 September 1992, p. i.
35. R. Matthews and T. Walker, 'Gulf Allies Impose "No-Fly" Zone in South Iraq', *Financial Times*, 27 August 1992.
36. P. Cockburn, 'Political Allies Turn On Bush', *Independent on Sunday*, 27 September 1992.
37. 'Arab Demurral Delays "No-Fly Zone"', *International Herald Tribune*, 25 August 1992; 'Arab Doubts Delay Allied Moves on Iraqi Air Exclusion Zone', *The Guardian*, 25 August 1992.
38. 'Bahrain: Military Cooperation Agreement Signed with UK', *Wakh*, 28 July 1992, *SWB* ME/1447, 31 July 1992, p. A/6; C. Bellamy, 'Arab States Refuse RAF Tornados', *Independent*, 25 August 1992.
39. See last paragraph of second section, entitled 'Visions of a New Era of Peace'.
40. 'Syrian Foreign Minister in Iran; Attempt to Mediate over Abu Musa', *SWB* ME/ 1491, 21 September 1992, p. i.
41. 'Egypt Proposes Rapid Deployment Force of Damascus Declaration States', *MENA*, 28 August 1992, *SWB* ME/1473, 31 August 1992, p. A/9.
42. 'Cairo Says Fate of Gulf Security Pact will be Decided Tomorrow', *Jordan Times*, 8 September 1992.
43. '"Practical Measures" Taken to Implement Damascus Declaration', *Arab Republic of Egypt Radio*, 11 September 1992, *SWB* ME/1484, 12 September 1992, p. A/3.
44. Text of statement issued at the conclusion of meetings of the Foreign Ministers of the GCC member states, Syria and Egypt, in Doha on 10 September 1992, *SWB* ME/1484, 12 September 1992, p. A/1.
45. *Ibid.*, p. A/2.

3. Boundaries in the Middle East

Julian Walker

INTRODUCTION

This chapter concerns the evolution and conflict potential of territorial boundaries in the Middle East from the Ottoman Empire to the present. In addition to consideration of Ottoman and European imperial legacies regarding frontier delimitation in the region, it focuses on the tensions caused by indigenous forces, themselves so often at odds with the Western concepts of the state and territorial limits. Consequently, the problem of frontiers in the Middle East has been as much about a clash of cultures as about traditional differences over pieces of territory.

BORDERS BEFORE THE FIRST WORLD WAR: THE OTTOMAN EMPIRE

The idea of fixed territorial borders is not native to the Middle East. Very few established boundaries existed there prior to the First World War, the prevailing system being that of the Ottoman Empire, ruled by a Sultan who was successor to the Muslim Caliphs. Muslims, under Turkish governors supported by Turkish garrisons, were predominant, and the position of the many racial and religious minorities was regulated by the millet system. As a result the main recognized boundaries were those of Ottoman control.

The boundary dividing Turkish rule from that of the Shahs of Persia, stretching from the Shatt al-Arab to the mountains of Kurdistan, had long been established, and was delimited just before the outbreak of war in 1914. The line between the Ottoman Empire and Egypt, where British and French interest was far stronger than that of Istanbul, stretched across the Sinai Peninsula. The Sanjak of Mount Lebanon, where European interest had dictated a special regime, was separated from the rest of Syria. And far to the south, where there were points of contact between Ottoman areas and those where the British had influence on the southern and eastern fringes of Arabia, some lines had been drawn. There had been demarcation of the frontier between Turkish Yemen and the tribes in treaty relations with the British masters of Aden, between the Bab al-Mandeb and Lakhmat al-Shuub in the Wadi Bana. But after that the dividing line became increasingly theoretical as it plunged into the Empty Quarter of the Arabian Peninsula along the Violet and Blue Lines until it emerged on the coast of the Persian Gulf at Zakhuniyah island.

Further north, around Kuwait, where British protection was entangled with Turkish suzerainty, the delimitation was far more precise, though the Anglo-Turkish Convention of 1913 which defined it, was never ratified. Elsewhere, in the centre of the Arabian Peninsula, where, despite Turkish incursions into al-Hasa and the Qasim in the 1870s, Ottoman power was never securely established, the supporters of Ibn Saud and Ibn Rashid vied for superiority and had little time for strange Western ideas of territorial limits. The internal divisions of Ottoman control into *vilayets* and *pashaliks* bore scant resemblance to the current rigid frontiers, or even to those of Europe in the earlier part of the 20th century.

THE POST-WAR FRONTIER SETTLEMENT AND THE ESTABLISHMENT OF THE MANDATE SYSTEM, 1918–30

The First World War, with the resultant collapse of the Ottoman Empire and the disappearance of the Caliphate, the Arab Revolt and the McMahon Letters, the Balfour Declaration and the Sykes–Picot Agreement, understandably resulted in a period of confusion. This was resolved during the first half of the 1920s, when Britain and France carved out their areas of mandate, obliterating Hashemite rule in Damascus and dividing up the Fertile Crescent. Aleppo lost its Mesopotamian hinterland. The French abandoned their claim to the Vilayet of Mosul in exchange for a short-lived domination of Cilicia, and made good their control of Deir al-Zor. The overall result was the creation of new administrative units including a truncated Syria and a newly swollen Lebanon incorporating Beirut. Palestine was deprived of its desert area, which was awarded to Shaikh Abdullah as his principality of Transjordan. And the three vilayets of Basra, Baghdad and Mosul combined to form the Kingdom of Iraq, compensating Faisal for his loss of Damascus. The Arab division of the Arabian Peninsula into Saudi Najd and Hasa, Hashemite Hejaz, Asir and the Imamate of Yemen, was left relatively undisturbed by the victors of the 1914–18 war.

The frontiers of the new states were then defined in a series of agreements. The borders between Iraq and Saudi Najd were settled at Uqair in 1922, when Saudi–Kuwaiti borders were also established. The Kuwaiti–Iraqi frontier (Schofield, 1991) of 1913 was confirmed in 1923. The Treaty of Lausanne laid the basis of the southern boundary of a resurgent Turkey with Syria and Iraq. The Hadda Agreement of 1925 delimited the frontier between the Saudis and the Jordanians. The League of Nations laboured to finalize the lines between Iraq and Syria, and then Iraq and Turkey, which were completed with the acceptance of the Brussels Line in 1926.

The settlement of these frontiers by no means signified the creation of Middle Eastern nation-states on the European model. The mandated territories were remarkable for the heterogeneity of the societies that they contained. In a memorandum written to his government in the early 1930s, Faisal, the first King of Iraq, summed up not only his own country's current, and continuing, problems of identity, but also those of Iraq's neighbours:

> This government rules over a Kurdish group most of which is ignorant and which includes persons with personal ambitions who call on this group to abandon government because it is not of their race. It also rules a Shia plurality which belongs to the same ethnic groups as the government... But as a result of the discriminations which the Shi'is incurred under Ottoman rule which did not allow them to participate in the affairs of government, a wide breach developed between these two sects. Unfortunately all this led the Shi'is... to abandon a government which they consider to be very bad... I discussed these great masses of the people without mentioning the other minorities, including Christian, which were encouraged to demand different rights. There are also other huge blocs of tribes... who want to reject everything related to government because of their interests and the ambitions of their shaikhs, whose powers recede if a government exists... I say with my heart full of sadness that there is not yet in Iraq an Iraqi people.

ACCEPTANCE OF THE MANDATE BORDERS

Despite the slowness with which these new frontiers encouraged the growth of Middle Eastern nation-states, they proved surprisingly uncontentious given the initial strangeness of the concept of such borders to local society. There were several possible reasons for this.

First, the very fact that the populations that they contained were so diverse and scattered meant that no frontier rectification could hope to achieve much improvement in the uniformity of the communities within the administrative area. Change might only have destabilized the fragile units which had been established by the original divisions, and threatened further disorder. Secondly, the prevailing belief in the Arab *umma*, the Arab nation or family, which was popular among Arab nationalists, encouraged demands for the abolition of all borders between Arabs, which, in theory at least, should not exist.

In addition, many of the new, straight-line borders ran through sparsely inhabited desert areas, far from the centres of population. Originally these frontiers were not strictly controlled and could be ignored by the great Bedu Arab tribes such as the Ruwalla, Shammar, Anaiza and Dulaim which regularly migrated across them. In certain areas neutral zones were established to cater for shared tribal grazing rights. Only where the new boundaries were controlled, and divided such tribes from their traditional market towns, as in Kuwait where there was trouble because of a Saudi economic blockade in the 1920s and Iraqi customs patrolling in the 1930s, did significant frontier incidents occur.

Finally, other frontiers passed through difficult countryside which formed natural barriers. Iraq's boundary in the north with Turkey and with Iran lay in Kurdish tribal mountain territory. There the authority of the central governments was weak and they attempted to bolster that authority through understandings with various tribal chiefs. These chiefs conducted their own feuds and friendships irrespective of the policies of the governments. Thus the positions of the frontiers, which often divided tribal areas, were regarded locally as having little relevance.

Consequently, the apparent ease with which the new borders were accepted belied actual circumstances. It gave the impression of the almost spontaneous emergence of coherent nationalities, united within a particular territorial context. Much of King Faisal's bleak assessment of the political realities in Iraq in the 1930s can be applied subsequently. It remains doubtful whether the people of Iraq, despite common sufferings in the war against Iran in the 1980s, the Gulf conflict and its aftermath, even now consider themselves an Iraqi nation. Indeed, such events have tended to expose and reinforce the divisions within Iraqi society.

The most contentious boundaries were often those which were close to ethnic divides. The difficulties which have resulted from the division of mandated Palestine between the Arabs and the Jews are well known. And even before the French surrender of the Hatay to Turkey the northern border of Syria was causing problems. Access was easy from both sides, and many Turkish Kurds who owned land north of the border shifted into Syria to escape the harsh attention of Atatürk's nationalist policies. Long negotiations were needed to resolve the problems. Elsewhere the southern section of the oldest Middle Eastern border of all, that between Iraq and Iran, continued to be an area of friction, not only because of Iranian rule over an Arab population in Mahommerah and Luristan, but also because of the increasingly congested waters of the Shatt al-Arab.

BORDERS IN THE ARABIAN PENINSULA AFTER 1930

Yemen–Aden

During the 1920s the Arabian Peninsula was for the most part untouched by Western efforts at frontier-drawing. The exception was the Yemeni hinterland of Aden, where the British attempted to consolidate the line they had agreed with the Turks, occupied Hodaida, and even gave sporadic support to the Idrisi ruler of Asir in the face of Imam Yahya, who was trying to eliminate their control of the tribes around Aden. He only relaxed his efforts in 1934, when he tacitly accepted the Anglo-Turkish line, which he considered unjust and imaginary, in order to leave his hands free to deal with a threat from the north. But the area remained troubled and the *status quo* agreed on by the two sides continued to be uncertain due, not least, to different Yemeni and British interpretations of the word 'frontiers' enshrined in the 1934 agreement.

Saudi–Yemen

The northern threat to Yahya arose out of Saudi elimination of the Kingdom of the Hejaz in 1925 and occupation of the Asir in the following year. The Imam had his own claims to the lands of the Idrisis of the Asir, itself an area from which the Imams had originated centuries before. The defeat of Imam Yahya's forces in the Tihama in 1934 led to the Treaty of Taif, and the subsequent demarcation of a Yemeni–Saudi boundary from Midi on the Red Sea coast to Buqa' in the neighbourhood of Najran. However, this line has remained unacceptable to most of the Yemeni public.

The persisting bitterness of the border dispute between the Yemenis and the Saudis is not born of ethnic differences. It arises from another traditional division in Arab society: the antagonism between the desert and the town, the traditional hostility between the settled townsmen and farmers of mountain territory, and the Bedu raiders from the sands. The Yemenis are proud of their ancient civilization and culture, the contribution of the Qahtanis of Yemeni origin to the Arab race, and the participation of Yemeni generals in the Arab conquest. They resent the haughtiness of the Saudis who they regard as *nouveau riche* Bedu of Adnani stock, and who, in Yemeni eyes, have no real past.

Oil Concessions and Tribes

In the remainder of the Arabian Peninsula the discovery of oil in Bahrain in 1932, followed by that in al-Hasa, aroused the interest of the Western world. The resultant scramble for oil concessions coincided with a period of Saudi–British negotiations over the boundaries around the periphery of the Empty Quarter, theoretically already bisected by the Blue and Violet Lines. Here expanding Saudi influence met that of the rulers of the British Protected States fringing the coastline between the Jabal Nakhsh in Qatar in the north and Aden in the south. In the Peninsula the Western concepts of nation-states, territorial sovereignty and fixed-line frontiers were even more alien to local ideas than they had been in the northern Middle East. The Arab Bedu tribes had been accustomed to roaming for hundreds of miles between their winter and their summer grazing. It was the men and their camels, or other livestock, that mattered rather than the comparatively barren land, which was valued basically for its pasture and its wells. The tribes switched their allegiance from one leader to another as their relationship with those leaders, and their hopes of gain as a result of their adherence to them, changed. Sometimes a tribe, or section of a tribe, would give tokens of fealty to two shaikhs at the same time. As a result the power of the leading families fluctuated continuously, as did the extent of their territorial influence.

British–Saudi Negotiations before the Second World War

In the 1930s and 1940s the power of King Abdulaziz of Saudi Arabia, Guardian of the Holy Places, waxed strong. He was not prepared to accept the Blue and Violet Lines, conceded to the British by the Turks after he had ousted the latter from al-Hasa. He had long had pretensions to a vague suzerainty over the shaikhs of the Trucial Coast, springing partly from his contempt for such insignificant rulers, and partly from an unwillingness to admit that an agreement he had made with the British at Jedda in 1927 precluded him from direct correspondence with them. Originally it appeared that he claimed the allegiance of the Murra, Bani Hajir and the Dimran, as well as part of the Manasir in the Empty Quarter. He also apparently demanded that the Manahil, (most of whom dwelt in the Hadramaut), the Al-Kathir of the same region, the Duru and the Awamir, who had sought the protection of Bin Jiluwi (his governor of al-Hasa, a decade earlier) be subject to his authority.

During the negotiations over Saudi Arabia's southern and eastern borders that followed, George Rendel, the leader of the British delegation, challenged the notion that frontiers could be defined on the basis of tribal areas alone. He agreed that certain areas of eastern Arabia were frequented, predominantly or exclusively, by tribes owing allegiance to one ruler or another, but argued that the areas under dispute were deserts over which several tribes wandered, whose allegiances were uncertain or shifting, and that a territorial frontier based on tribal considerations alone would be impracticable. However, he agreed that there was no question of attempting to establish a sharply defined frontier in the European sense. But some territorial limit beyond which sovereignty could not be exercised had to be laid down, even if such sovereignty was not, in fact, exercised up to that limit. This would not prevent tribes wandering freely from one territory to another, and it was anticipated that suitable taxation and other administrative arrangements could be made as had been done in the case of the tribes which migrated between Saudi Arabia, Transjordan, Syria and Iraq.

In 1934 Rendel proposed a desert zone in the Empty Quarter of the Arabian Peninsula which would have a special regime for a decade, involving the surrender of all territorial sovereignty and the right to grant economic concessions, with arrangements for the reliance on tribal authority alone, and for the control of disturbances. However, ultimately the idea was abandoned when it became clear that the area it would have covered was too small for such complicated arrangements to be practical.

Buraimi–Akhdar

Eventually these negotiations came to nothing, although they succeeded in laying down general parameters for future frontiers, between the Fuad Hamza and the Riyadh Lines, which were put forward by the opposing parties in 1935. They were thwarted not because of disagreement over the desert wastes of the Empty Quarter, but because of rival claims to the relatively small features of Jabal Nakhsh and the Khor al-Odaid. Failure to reach agreement before the outbreak of the Second World War stored up trouble for the future.

After 1949 tension between Saudi Arabia and the coastal states developed into the Buraimi dispute. This was exacerbated by the arrival of a Saudi representative in the Buraimi oasis where the Ruler of Abu Dhabi and the Sultan of Muscat divided sovereignty between them. The Saudis were finally evicted from the oasis in October 1955 after an attempt at arbitration had collapsed, but not before their attempts to spread their influence had fostered further troubles in the interior of Oman which put the Imam of the Ibadhis at odds with the Sultan on the coast. These troubles lasted until January 1959, when, after the storming of the Jabal Akhdar, the Imam took refuge with Bin Jiluwi in al-Hasa in eastern Saudi Arabia.

Pacification of the Omani Interior

Until this unrest attracted attention to them, the territories in the interior of the Trucial States and the Sultanate of Oman had remained a tribal backwater, hardly visited by the British since the beginning of the century (Schofield, 1993). In Oman the Agreement of Sib in 1920, and the financial difficulties of the Sultan of Muscat, had prevented the latter from consolidating his suzerainty over the tribes of the interior. In the Trucial States the collapse of the pearl trade in the early 1930s had left the shaikhs of the coast desperately poor, and with little control over the tribes and the slave traders roaming inland. The war between Abu Dhabi and Dubai of the late 1940s had added to the lack of security in the area, even if, at the end of it, the British had imposed a stretch of border – the first definitive frontier in south-eastern Arabia – between the two shaikhdoms, running south-eastwards from the coast at Ras Hasian. After that the measures taken to prevent Saudi penetration radically altered the situation in the interior.

The Trucial–Oman Levies were founded in 1951 to combat slave-trading and to protect British officials and oil company personnel. They were expanded rapidly in 1952 to support the forces of the Ruler of Abu Dhabi and the Sultan of Muscat in blockading the Saudis in Buraimi. By 1954 their patrols had established relative security in the Trucial States, Buraimi and the Dhahira north of Ibri. Then the Sultan of Muscat sent his forces northwards from his southern coast, escorting a party of oil prospectors who wished to drill at Fahud in Duru tribal territory. Under pressure from the Duru some of these forces advanced to the tribe's market town of Ibri, linking up with the Levies. The Sultan's control over the gravel plains to the east of inner Oman was consolidated, and the interior opened up for oil exploration. In August 1955, when the arrangements for arbitration collapsed two months before the Saudis were expelled from the Buraimi oasis, the British announced, unilaterally, the frontier which they would hitherto regard as the border between Saudi Arabia on the one hand, and Abu Dhabi, Oman and the Aden Protectorate on the other.

Trucial States Settlement

In 1954, with the exception of the Ruler of Abu Dhabi who had been incensed by the imposition on him of a frontier with Dubai at Ras Hasian, the rulers of the Trucial Coast, anxious for oil income to escape the poverty which had afflicted their shaikhdoms since the collapse of the pearl trade, agreed to British arbitration over their frontiers. By the end of 1957 the British had decided on a network of irregular lines, established on the basis of local history, tribal custom and frequent consultation with the disputing parties (Schofield, 1993). The patch-work quilt of intermingling territories which resulted was both illogical and impossible from the Western viewpoint. Of the six states involved, only one, Umm al-Qawain, had a consolidated territory. Of the rest Sharjah was divided into six enclaves, and tiny Ajman into three. Dubai had two, as did the mutually antagonistic Fujairah and Ras al-Khaimah who shared a zone where they were awarded shared rights. Though odd, this settlement accorded with local perceptions. It has survived in its basic form, and has even been added to by completion of the frontiers of Abu Dhabi with Dubai and Sharjah, the former embellished with a further neutral zone. Nevertheless it could not have worked without the spirit of co-operation that had grown up between the rulers of the Trucial Coast. This led the latter to declare their union in the United Arab Emirates (UAE) when the British withdrew in 1971. However, the frontiers between the Emirates have not been obliterated by that union.

Trucial States–Oman

The British also helped tackle the question of the frontier between the Trucial States and Oman in the late 1950s and early 1960s (Schofield, 1993). With the exception of a small section near the boundary with the Saudis which the British had announced in August 1955, the longest stretch of this line, namely that between Abu Dhabi and the Sultanate, was agreed by 1960, along with shorter sections between Ajman, Dubai, Fujairah and the Sultanate. Traditional Qawasim–Muscat rivalry delayed settlement between the Sultanate and Sharjah and Ras al-Khaimah, but a *modus vivendi* was reached by Sharjah in the 1960s. Also, in recent years Shaikh Saqr of Ras al-Khaimah has indicated that he has come to an understanding with Sultan Sayid Qabus, even though there may be some minor difficulties outstanding between them over some of the mountainous Shihuh territory of Ruus al-Jibal.

Saudi Arabia–UAE–Oman

The line that the British declared as the boundary of Abu Dhabi, Oman and the Eastern Protectorate with Saudi Arabia in August 1955 was intentionally a compromise line, produced in the hope that the Saudis might come to accept it, in later years, as a reasonable border (Schofield, 1993). It was essentially the Riyadh Line of 1935, modified in the light of a further 20 years of knowledge of the area. British hopes were largely fulfilled. The line was further changed by negotiation between Shaikh Zaid of Abu Dhabi and King Faisal of Saudi Arabia in 1974, and although the modifications have not been made public, this changed line is generally acknowledged as the border between them. In 1991 the Sultan of Oman and King Fahd sank their differences and accepted the 1955 line as the boundary dividing their two states.

Only that section of the border between the old Eastern Aden Protectorate and Saudi Arabia, part of which was subject to armed clashes between forces of the Saudi Kingdom and the People's Democratic Republic of Yemen (PDRY) in 1971, remains disputed. Its extension north and west to the point where the line demarcated under the 1934 Treaty of Taif ended at Buqa, is also undefined and a source of friction.

On the other hand, the frontier dividing the two Yemens, which caused so much friction between the British and the Imam, and thereafter between the PDRY and the Republic of Yemen in the 1970s and 1980s, disappeared with the union of the two Yemens in May 1990. This latter event encouraged hope of agreement on the long undefined frontier between Yemen and the Sultanate of Oman's province of Dhofar.

CONCLUSION

Thus the process of the delimitation of frontiers in the Middle East, initiated basically by the Anglo-Ottoman Conventions of 1913 and 1914, is drawing to an end. The main borders that continue to fester are well known. In the north the ethnic boundaries of Israel and its occupied territories, and between Iran and Iraq, preoccupy the United Nations. The UN is also involved with the demarcation of the Kuwait–Iraq border. In the south there are problems outstanding between Saudi Arabia and Yemen, and Qatar and Bahrain.

All the 20th century boundaries of the Middle East are artificial, almost as artificial as those of Africa which were settled by imperial agreements at the end of the 19th century. In the northern Middle East they were dictated basically by the administrative and political *desiderata* of the mandatory powers, Britain and France, even if the needs of the tribes, and the standards of the League of Nations, played a role in their delineation. In the south the frontiers tended to rigidify the traditional ebb and flow of influence of various ruling families over the tribes, freezing what had been a cyclical process at a certain point in time. The Mandates have disappeared, and the power of the tribes is vanishing rapidly. On the edge of the Empty Quarter there are few people who now worry whether the wells of Sufuk, or of the Kidan, belong to the Murra or the Manasir. While new bore holes have been drilled, the tribal young are mostly in the cities drinking desalinated water. Even the camel has become the adjunct of shaikhly racing.

The present frontier disputes among the states of the Gulf Co-operation Council (GCC) are largely dynastic problems. The basis of power has shifted from the allegiance of the Bedu to the wealth which arises from oil production, itself decided by the possession of territory. The quarrel between Qatar and Bahrain over the Hawar Islands, Fasht al-Jaradah and Fasht al-Dibal, is mainly one between the Al-Khalifa and the Al-Thani, exacerbated by hopes of oil under the surrounding seabed. The ruling families of the UAE continue to bicker over borders of which their subjects are largely unaware. The recent stresses in Saudi–Qatari relations seem to have arisen because of Al-Thani rejection of Saudi mediation over Hawar, and of Saudi rein-pulling in dealing with Tehran over the shared North Dome Field. The populations of most of the Gulf states are more concerned about the fortunes of their national football teams than the possession of sand dunes and shallows.

In the past the shaikhs did not regard a written and signed piece of paper with the same reverence as the Westerner, let alone a Western lawyer. A written contract, including one which defined borders, was understood to indicate the attitudes of the parties to it at the moment it was concluded, rather than to be an undertaking fixed forever in time. The rigidity of the West could not encompass the flexibility of the East, where Allah, not man, disposes. But the West now seems to have succeeded in imposing its rigidity on the East. Western lawyers profit from boundary disputes between the rulers and help decide the outcome. The Kingdom of the Hejaz could not now disappear, as it did in 1925, without Security Council debates, resolutions, UN observers and the possibility of a reversal of the process. Attempts to change frontiers by force in the Middle East, whether in Palestine, Kuwait or even on the Shatt al-Arab, have led to widespread international involvement. The Kurds, who have a greater sense of nationhood than did the populations of Transjordan and Iraq in 1920, continue to yearn, with little hope, for a state and frontiers of their own.

The Middle East remains unsettled, and takes a large amount of UN time. Without the present frontiers the situation could well have been much worse. As has been indicated, those frontiers were largely based on alien factors, or ones which are losing their relevance in modern Middle Eastern society. Nevertheless, their very existence has shaped the development of that society. It remains to be seen whether the Western system of nation-states, overseen by the international community, is more acceptable to the Middle East than that of the Ottoman Empire with its Muslim Caliph, Turkish governors, Sunni dominance, and millet system. Will it last as long?

4. Water and politics in the Middle East

Greg Shapland

INTRODUCTION

This chapter concerns the competition for water between states in the Middle East, and the consequent disputes, both actual and potential.

Among the areas in the Middle East affected by competition between states for water supplies, the Nile and Tigris–Euphrates basins and water issues in the Arab–Israel dispute are three of the most significant. The first two of these are major river basins by any standards, and also areas of ancient civilizations based on irrigated agriculture. The third is, in geographical terms, a minor river basin, consisting of the River Jordan and its tributaries, and a number of rain-fed aquifers in Israel and the occupied territories.

THE NILE BASIN

Egypt and much of northern Sudan depend almost entirely on the Nile for water for agricultural, industrial and domestic needs (see Figure 4.1). But their contribution to the flow of the river is negligible: the waters of the Nile are derived essentially from rainfall on the Ethiopian highlands and the region of the central African lakes. Some 86 per cent of the flow of the main Nile, below Khartoum, comes from the Ethiopian highlands, principally from the Blue Nile, but also from the Sobat. The relatively small contribution of the White Nile is explained by the enormous losses in the swamps of southern Sudan (see Waterbury, 1979 and Shahin, 1985). The civil war there has brought to a halt the construction of the Jonglei Canal, a project designed to reduce these losses (see Howell, Lock and Cobb, 1989).

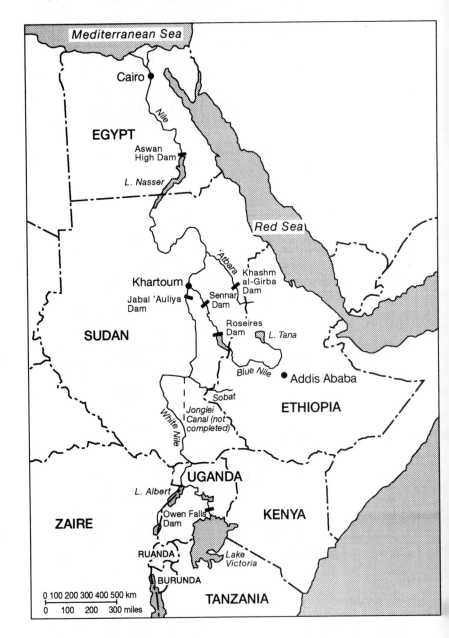

Figure 4.1   The Nile basin

There are substantial variations in the flow of the Nile from year to year. The Aswan High Dam, which was completed in 1971, has given Egypt the capacity to even out available water supplies from one year to the next. It cannot, however, provide complete protection against a long run of years of low flow such as occurred during the 1980s. There are several sizeable dams in Sudan, which impound water for irrigation and hydro-power. The Owen Falls Dam on the White Nile in Uganda generates hydro-power. Elsewhere in the Nile basin, little has been done to regulate the river. Money is short and, with the exception of Ethiopia, the need is much less pressing owing to higher rainfall.

An agreement signed by Egypt and Sudan in 1959 made possible the construction of the Aswan High Dam, and apportioned the average flow of the Nile between the two states in the ratio of 3:1 in favour of Egypt.[1] The agreement has been faithfully applied, whatever the political climate between Egypt and Sudan (Waterbury, 1979).

No comprehensive agreement involving all nine states of the Nile basin has ever been signed. Nor is there any organization grouping all the nine states that could provide a forum for discussions which could lead to such an agreement. A number of bodies deal with particular technical aspects of the river, but none seems suited to talks on water-sharing. The Undugu Group, set up on Egyptian initiative in 1983, periodically brings together most of the nine – but not Ethiopia or Kenya – for talks on economic and political issues. But although the Group's communiqués refer to the Nile in general terms, its discussions of the subject do not seem to have gone very far.

Even in years of good rainfall, Ethiopia is unable to feed its 50 million people, and faces famine in poor years. It lacks foreign currency to pay for food imports. The Ethiopians are likely, therefore, to want to store the waters of the Blue Nile or its tributaries for irrigation, as a means of increasing agricultural production and insuring against drought. However, the Ethiopians lack the money with which to exploit their country's considerable potential for irrigation. But if money were to become available, they could not be expected to accept Egypt's claims to 'historic rights' as a constraint on their own exploitation of the river.

Southern Sudan receives sufficient rainfall to make irrigation unnecessary. But the north of the country is far drier, and needs Nile water both for domestic water and power generation, and to irrigate the major agricultural projects which provide over half of Sudan's foreign exchange earnings. Sudan is therefore vulnerable to increased use of water by upstream states. At the same time it represents a potential threat to Egypt. There is considerable scope for the further development of irrigated agriculture in Sudan, which could mean using water now being consumed by Egypt: in the 1970s, Sudan had ambitious plans to become the 'bread-basket of the Arab world', but these have so far come to nothing through a combination of incompetence and corruption.

The Egyptians already use all of the water allocated to them under their agreement with Sudan. They have had to struggle to remain within the quota. The vulnerability of their water supplies was brought home to them by the drought of the 1980s. By the summer of 1988, the government had been forced to restrict the area under rice – Egypt's most demanding crop in terms of water – and the generating plants at the Aswan Dam were operating at less than two-thirds of capacity, constituting a loss of around 7 per cent of the country's total power production capacity.[2] Lake Nasser fell almost to the level at which no electricity could have been generated at the Dam, although the high flood later in the year restored its generating capacity.

Egypt's population – already 56 million – is growing rapidly, at 2.4 per cent per annum, adding a million new mouths every nine months. Even if the upstream states undertook to do nothing which would affect the flow of water into Lake Nasser, Egypt would still face mounting difficulties in meeting its rising demand for water for agriculture, industry and domestic consumption.

Nevertheless, the picture for Egypt is not entirely bleak. There are a number of measures which the Egyptians could take, or are already taking, to make better use of the water they receive or to reduce consumption. The possibilities for saving water are great: by reducing waste in domestic and industrial use; by adopting modern irrigation methods; and by allowing less water to escape unused to the Mediterranean. Major savings of water could be made if the ambitious programme of desert reclamation using Nile water were cut back. This seems unlikely, however, as the government sees reclamation as the answer to overcrowding and unemployment in the cities (Foreign and Commonwealth Office, 1990).

A programme of building new power-stations, begun in the late 1980s, is making Egypt less dependent on the Nile for its electricity. Indeed, less than 10 per cent of Egypt's electricity is now generated at Aswan. Family planning to lower the rate of population growth is being promoted by the government, and may be starting to have some effect.

Recently discovered aquifers beneath the deserts west of the Nile could be exploited, if the costs are not too high: although their exact extent is not known, they appear to be huge. Because of its present cost and the enormous quantities of water Egypt requires, desalination does not seem to be an option in the foreseeable future.

Externally, Egypt could take steps to counter the potential threat to its water supplies posed by developments upstream. It could block funding from international agencies, which will not lend if other riparians object: in company with Sudan, Egypt has vetoed funding for an Ethiopian irrigation project (Foreign and Commonwealth Office, 1990; Krishna, 1992). By using its political clout, Egypt could also discourage funding from individual donor states. Given their poverty, the upstream states are unlikely to be able to undertake significant projects on their own in the foreseeable future.

The Egyptians should thus have a breathing-space in which they can work through diplomacy to obtain water-sharing agreements with upstream riparians. These states are, however, in no hurry to close their options by agreeing to take fixed quantities of water that might eventually prove to be insufficient. They are unwilling to enter negotiations until they see that it is in their interest to do so. For the moment, therefore, a more realistic goal for Egyptian diplomacy is to dissuade upstream states from works which would seriously reduce Egypt's supply of Nile water. The most important states in this context are Sudan and Ethiopia, being the greatest potential users.

The Egyptians appear to despair of any real improvement in relations with the present regime in Khartoum. They could be expected, however, to try to establish a close relationship with any successor regime, and to work for a solution to the civil war in southern Sudan. Such a solution would permit the completion of the Jonglei Canal, making significantly greater quantities of water available to both Egypt and Sudan (Collins, 1990).

During the later years of the Mengistu era, the Egyptians made efforts – to some extent successful – to improve relations with Ethiopia. This has continued since Mengistu's fall. For their part, the Ethiopians now appear to want a much closer relationship with Egypt. The reactivation of the Egypt–Ethiopia Joint Commission was announced in February 1992. President Zenawi may see Egypt as an intermediary with potential benefactors. In return for assistance in such areas, the Egyptians would almost certainly seek some kind of Ethiopian assurances over the Nile.

Outlook

The demands on Nile water will inevitably rise. There is rapid population growth – between 2.4 and 4 per cent per annum – in all states of
the basin. This will lead to higher demand for water, not only for direct
consumption but also for irrigation, although given the dominance of
agriculture in the economies of the states of the basin, with the exception of Egypt, industrial consumption will not increase significantly in
the foreseeable future.

Egypt apart, Sudan and Ethiopia have the greatest potential for irrigated agriculture. A major expansion in Sudan would result in a considerable reduction in the amount of water available to Egypt, and could
lead the Sudanese to call for the renegotiation of the 1959 agreement.
Greater use of water by Ethiopia, where the scope for dam-building is
greatest, could cause reductions in flow to both Sudan and Egypt.[3]

The Sudanese, and particularly the Egyptians, would find it hard to
accept control of the Blue Nile by Ethiopia, at least in the absence of an
agreement guaranteeing their supplies. In times of drought, Ethiopia
would be in a position to withhold water from both Sudan and Egypt,
whether to satisfy its own needs or as leverage. But Egypt should be
able to prevent such a situation arising in the foreseeable future, either
by diplomatic persuasion or by blocking funding for Ethiopian water
projects.

As long as such measures prove effective, the Egyptians are most
unlikely to threaten, and even more unlikely to use, force to prevent
unwelcome developments upstream. The late President Sadat publicly
declared on a number of occasions during 1980 that Egypt would go to
war to stop Ethiopia from obstructing Egypt's plans to channel Nile
water to Sinai. Since his death, however, these threats have not been
repeated, although remarks by the Egyptian Defence Minister in an
interview in October 1991 indicate that the idea remains in Egyptian
minds – or perhaps that the Egyptians want upstream states to believe
that it does.[4]

THE TIGRIS–EUPHRATES BASIN

The Tigris and Euphrates both rise in the mountains of eastern Anatolia
(see Figure 4.2). Nearly all the Euphrates flow is generated in Turkey,
with just over one-tenth added in Syria and a negligible amount in Iraq.

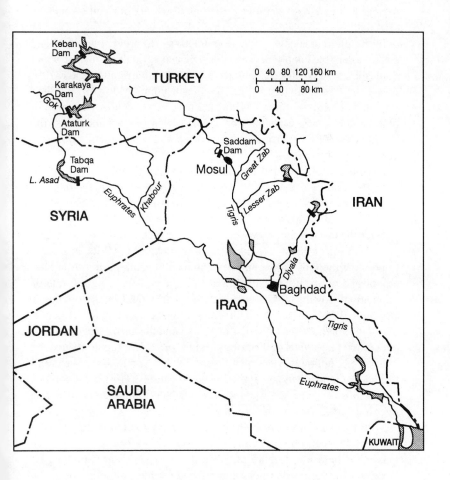

Figure 4.2   The Tigris–Euphrates basin

The flow of the Tigris is less susceptible to Turkish control: only half of its water originates in Turkey, with the balance coming from Iraq's northern mountains.

As with most rivers in semi-arid countries, the flow of these two varies with the season, with the peak coming in the spring. From year to year there are considerable variations which are difficult to manage effectively.

In these circumstances storage is important to prevent flooding and ensure a reliable supply of water for irrigated agriculture, industry and domestic use. Syria uses Euphrates water for both irrigation and hydro-power: its principal work is the Tabqa Dam, completed in 1976, which impounds Lake Asad. Iraq has constructed a large number of dams and other water works, especially on the Tigris and its tributaries: in the Euphrates valley the terrain is less favourable for the creation of reservoirs.

In contrast to Syria and lowland Iraq, eastern Anatolian agriculture has until recently been mostly rain-fed. Turkey's interest in the region's rivers was earlier focused mainly on their hydro-power potential, which the Keban and Karakaya Dams were built to exploit.

Over the last decade, however, Turkey has elaborated the South-east Anatolia Project. Known by its Turkish acronym of GAP, its purpose is to promote the rapid economic development of south-eastern Anatolia, a poor and politically-sensitive area with the country's highest rate of population growth. If fully realized, the GAP would involve the construction of 22 dams and 18 hydro-power plants, enabling the irrigation of 1.5 million hectares of agricultural land and the annual generation of over 6,500 megawatts of electricity (Bagis 1989). This could reduce the volume of Euphrates water available to Syria by up to 40 per cent and to Iraq by 60 per cent, and also increase its salinity. The largest component of this project is the Ataturk Dam, which is to impound a reservoir over four times the volume of Lake Asad.

With the populations of both Syria and Iraq expected to double over the next 18 years, both countries have strong reasons for wanting to maximize the use of Euphrates water. Syria in particular is pinning its hopes on future development along the Euphrates, although progress there has been slow so far due to financial and technical circumstances, the latter being mainly to do with poor soil quality. Little information is available concerning Iraq's plans for the Euphrates; but it will inevitably require more water for irrigation. The United Nations embargo has strengthened Iraq's desire for greater self-sufficiency in food production, reflected in the emphasis placed by Saddam on the 'Third River' project. Iraq's largest dam project, the Saddam Dam, is on the Tigris, the flow of which is less threatened by Turkish plans.

Until the implications of Turkey's GAP became clear, most of the wrangling over the Euphrates was between Iraq and Syria, exacerbating the long-standing rivalry between the two regimes. An example of the hostility between Baghdad and Damascus came in April 1975 when Iraq moved troops on its border with Syria and threatened to bomb the Tabqa Dam. The issue was defused in large part by Saudi mediation (Kienle, 1990). Syrian–Iraqi differences and Iraq's preoccupation with its war with Iran prevented any progress in the Euphrates Technical Committee comprising Turkey, Syria and Iraq, established in the early 1980s. There are also differences between the two Arab states and Turkey on the Committee's terms of reference, with Iraq and Syria pressing for discussion of water volumes, and Turkey preferring to stick to technical questions.

Syria and Iraq were eventually driven towards co-operation when the Turks announced in November 1989 that they would stop the flow of the Euphrates at the Atatürk Dam for a month from mid-January 1990 in order to begin filling the reservoir, and indeed did so.[5] The Turks said they would permit a higher flow both before and after this stoppage, so that Syria and Iraq could maintain the levels of their own reservoirs. Meanwhile the flow from the River Gok would enable Turkey to meet the commitment which it had made in 1987 to maintain the average annual flow of at least 500 cubic metres per second into Syria. In April 1990 the two Arab states agreed that Syria would allow Iraq 58 per cent of the flow of the Euphrates at the Turkish–Syrian border.

The two Arab states together pressed Turkey to guarantee them fixed quotas of Euphrates water above 500 cubic metres per second, and Iraq laid claim to 700 cubic metres per second. The Turks have, however, firmly resisted national quotas, arguing for the joint development of the whole Tigris–Euphrates basin. No progress was made, and the emerging Arab front collapsed with the Gulf crisis.

Even without the hostility between Iraq and Syria, Turkey would be in a strong position. It controls all the sources of the water required for the GAP. Turkey is funding the GAP from its own resources, having been refused loans from the World Bank because of the objections of the downstream states. Nor are Turkey's plans affected by availability of hard currency, since the contractors are paid in Turkish lira. Syria's loss of superpower backing with the demise of the Soviet Union and

Iraq's defeat in the Gulf War have further reduced any threat to Turkey. Nonetheless, Turkey has an interest in commercial relations with both Syria and Iraq, and will want to sell agricultural produce and electricity from the GAP to Arab states.

In seeking to justify greater use of the Euphrates, the Turks have adduced the needs of the large population of south-eastern Anatolia. They have also pointed to the fact that their works will enable better control of variations in flow. Moreover, the Turks are correct in arguing that it is more sensible to store water in the mountains of Anatolia, where evaporation losses are low, than in the lowlands downstream. The further Turkish claim that Syrian and Iraqi irrigation methods are wasteful is also correct, although the techniques which the Turks plan to use in the GAP are far from being the most efficient available. It is harder to assess Turkish assertions that Syria and Iraq exaggerate their water needs, but it would be natural for them to do so in advance of possible negotiations.

Of the three countries in the Tigris–Euphrates basin, Syria is the worst placed. It has no other major developed sources of water, and the Euphrates system is crucial to its economy. Power generation has already been hard hit by temporarily reduced flows in the Euphrates, caused by periodic droughts.

Furthermore, Syria lacks the capacity to earn hard currency from oil or other exports on the scale normally enjoyed by Iraq (when not interrupted by the Gulf crisis and sanctions) which could be spent on food imports if water shortages forced substantial cut-backs in domestic agricultural production. Syria has no direct leverage on Turkey, and has no control over the flow of water from Turkey. Bilateral relations are uneasy, partly because of the Turks' belief that Syria is supporting the Kurdish Workers' Party (the PKK) which poses a serious security threat within Turkey, particularly in the south-east.[6] Iraq can make up some of the shortfall from Turkish and Syrian use of the Euphrates with water from the Tigris and its tributaries. Turkey's plans for the Tigris are less ambitious than for the Euphrates and are also less advanced. Water from those tributaries of the Tigris which rise in the high mountains on the Iraq–Iran border will of course be unaffected. Nonetheless, Iraq's agriculture is likely to be hard hit by pollution in the Euphrates, as the water used for irrigation in Turkey and Syria will reach Iraqi land with higher concentrations of chemicals and salts. Iraq already faces serious problems of salinity, which have rendered large areas of farmland unusable.

Outlook

Economic development and population growth will increase Syria's demand for water, while Turkey's GAP will reduce the quantity available. Syria is likely to suffer growing shortages of water for agriculture and domestic use, and electricity generation will be impaired. The Syrians may try to develop other sources of water and to use it more efficiently. It is unlikely that they will push their grievance over the Euphrates to the point of confrontation with Turkey. They probably realize that this would be counter-productive.

It is difficult to forecast Iraq's demand for water in the near future. The pressure on the Iraqi regime's hard currency reserves is likely for some time to translate into greater requirements for locally produced food and hence for water, to keep down imports. In the longer term, reconstruction in Iraq should mean that demand for water will increase. Whatever regime is in power in Baghdad, Iraq is likely to protest about Turkish abstraction from, and pollution of, the Euphrates. The Iraqis may also round on the Syrians if they maintain their abstractions at Iraq's expense – as they did during the dry summer of 1989.

Turkey has proposed a two-pronged 'peace pipeline' to bring water from the Seyhan and Ceyhan, wholly Turkish rivers, to Syria and the Arabian Peninsula (Parker, 1991). This could help to make up for reductions in the flow of the Euphrates caused by the GAP. But Syria and the Arab states would have to purchase the water on commercial terms, and have so far shown little enthusiasm.

The Turks are behind with the GAP owing to financial difficulties. The current forecast for completion is 2005, but some elements of the project will probably take much longer. There will be periods of friction before then as the Turks fill reservoirs by reducing the flow of the Euphrates and the Tigris, although the latter will be less serious. Syria and Iraq will protest loudly, may try to retaliate commercially, and may seek arbitration or the mediation of other states. But they will probably be unable to do anything to prevent the Turks from going ahead with their plans.

WATER ISSUES IN THE ARAB–ISRAEL DISPUTE

Israel's two main sources of water are the Sea of Galilee, fed by the River Jordan and its tributaries, and the aquifers lying beneath the West

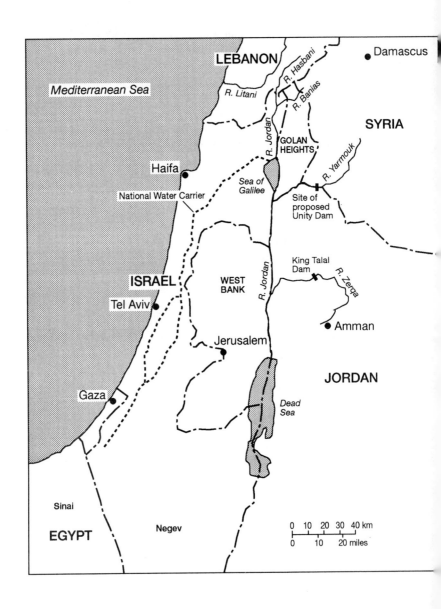

Figure 4.3   The Jordan basin

Bank and the coastal plain (see Figure 4.3). Apart from the main coastal aquifer, Israel shares these sources with others: with Jordan, Lebanon and Syria in the case of the River Jordan and all but one of its main tributaries, namely the Dan; and with the occupied territories in the case of the aquifers beneath the West Bank and Gaza.

In the early 1960s, Israel constructed the National Water Carrier, which conveys 400 million cubic metres of water a year, in years of normal rainfall, from the Sea of Galilee to the populous coastal plain, including Tel Aviv, and beyond to the arid Negev region, for irrigation and domestic and industrial use (Tahal, 1990). Syria has built a number of small dams on the Yarmouk and its tributaries. Jordan built the King Talal Dam on the Zerqa in the early 1970s. But Jordan's most ambitious project, the construction of the Unity Dam on the Yarmouk (which was to have been undertaken jointly with Syria), has been blocked by Israeli objections and its usefulness called into question by Syrian abstractions upstream.

The aquifers which Israel shares with the Palestinians are tapped by wells. Israeli wells are generally deeper than those sunk by the Palestinians, and are operated by pumps with a higher capacity. Although the West Bank aquifers extend into Israel, most of the rainfall which replenishes them falls on the hills of the West Bank. Before 1967, Israel was already able to abstract some 300 million cubic metres a year from wells situated just within Israel (Pearce, 1991). Since the West Bank came under their control in 1967, the Israelis have imposed severe restrictions on increases in abstractions of water by Palestinians. Meanwhile, the Israelis have drilled new wells there to supply Jewish settlements, although most of the West Bank water used by Israel still comes from wells sunk in pre-1967 Israel. Israel is now taking more than 90 per cent of the water drawn from the West Bank aquifers (Shuval, 1992).

Israel currently depends on water from the West Bank, whether tapped there or within its pre-1967 boundaries, for around 25 per cent of its total consumption. Another 10 per cent of this consumption may be derived from tributaries of the Jordan which rise in the Golan Heights.

In Jordan, Israel and the occupied territories, between 65 and 80 per cent of the water supply is consumed by agriculture. Throughout the area there is a drive to increase agricultural production. This results partly from a desire for export earnings, while 'food security' remains an important consideration. But rapid population growth plays a large part too: if greater imports of food and consequent balance-of-payments difficulties are to be avoided, new mouths must be fed by production at home. In Israel, the rate of natural increase among the Jewish population is only 2 per cent per annum, but immigration from the Soviet Union pushed the overall rate of growth up to 6.4 per cent in 1990. In the West Bank and the Gaza Strip the annual rates of growth are 3.1 and 3.6 per cent, respectively – among the highest in the world – while Jordan's rate (hitherto of 3.6 per cent) rose to 4.7 per cent in 1991 as a result of the mass return of Palestinians from the Gulf. Domestic consumption of water is growing quickly – in Jordan, at a steady 10 per cent per annum during the second half of the 1980s. Industrialization is further increasing demand.

Precipitation during the winter of 1991–92 was exceptional. But it has only brought temporary relief. A further run of dry years would bring renewed difficulties. Until the winter of 1991–92, both Israel and Jordan were using between 10 and 15 per cent more water each year than was being replenished by rainfall: it seemed likely that, given average rainfall, abstraction at present rates would exhaust the West Bank aquifers soon after the turn of the century.

Before the winter of 1991–92, water shortages in Israel prompted the government to introduce restrictions on water use in agriculture. Measures of this kind will have to be reinstated and eventually strengthened: there are no untapped sources of water within Israel or the occupied territories to which Israel can turn. A portion of the Litani in southern Lebanon lies within the Israeli 'security zone' but, despite persistent rumours, there is no evidence that Israel is secretly tapping this river by a tunnel dug into the river bed. The Israelis have tried a variety of sophisticated techniques to make more water available or make better use of what they already have; but so far the benefits do not appear to be keeping pace with the growth in demand. As Israel lacks cheap energy, desalination has proved prohibitively expensive except where, as in Eilat, no alternative is available.

Jordan is also suffering from water shortages. A Jordanian official said in September 1991 that, by 1990, demand had outstripped supply by 35 million cubic metres, or about 5 per cent of the country's total supply. He claimed that this deficit had since then been doubled by the influx of Palestinians from the Gulf. Rationing has been introduced throughout the country. The Jordanians are making efforts to improve efficiency in irrigation. They are also investigating new sources. But without a significant improvement in supply, Jordan's water crisis can only deepen.

The coastal aquifer on which the Gaza Strip's 700,000 inhabitants rely is being consumed 50 per cent faster than it is being replenished. At the present rate of depletion, it will be unable by the end of the century to supply enough water for domestic and industrial use, let alone agriculture. There has already been some intrusion of sea-water into the aquifer, which has also been contaminated as a result of the inadequacies of the sewage system. On the West Bank, over-pumping by Israelis has lowered the water-table to the point where some Palestinian wells have run dry (United Nations, 1992).

WATER AND THE MADRID PEACE CONFERENCE

Water 'rights' form one element of the bilateral talks between Israel and the Arabs, whilst co-operation over water is being tackled by one of the multilateral working groups on regional issues. The ideal outcome of these talks would be the introduction of a regional water management plan, along the lines of the Johnston Plan, a scheme for the development of the water resources of the entire Jordan basin, promoted by the US in the 1950s. These efforts foundered, mainly because of the unwillingness of certain Arab leaders to contemplate any agreement that could be seen as contributing to Israel's development. Until recent years, however, at least Jordan and Israel tacitly observed the main provisions of the Johnston Plan, only ceasing to do so under the pressure of increased demand.

Such an arrangement would improve the prospects for containing the water crisis, although it would not be enough to resolve it: to achieve this, it may be necessary to bring water into the region from elsewhere, probably from Turkey. The absence of any universally accepted body of international law on the subject that could act as a framework will be a significant handicap. But agreement is in any event unlikely whilst the parties distrust each other so strongly. They will see such negotiations, at least initially, as an exercise in which any gain by others would be a loss to them. Until progress has been made towards a political settlement between the parties, co-operation over water will be very difficult to achieve. The policy of the Syrians and Lebanese has been to refuse to attend any of the multilateral meetings, including those on water, until progress has been made in the bilateral talks.

To date, progress on water issues has been no faster than in other areas of the peace process. Water has only recently received explicit mention on the agenda of the bilateral talks between Israel and Jordan – itself a big step forward – but has not received simultaneous attention in the other bilateral talks. Progress in the multilateral talks has been slow. Overall, the Palestinians and the Arab states have demonstrated a reluctance to embark on co-operative ventures with Israel until agreement is much closer in the bilateral talks.

In any case, the Arabs' preference is to discuss the water 'rights' aspect, where they probably feel that Israel's much higher per capita consumption gives them a strong negotiating position. From the strictly economic point of view, Israel would find it difficult but not impossible to make some concessions: agriculture, the greatest consumer of water, now only accounts for some 3 per cent of Israel's GNP, and employs under 5 per cent of the work-force. But agriculture is central to Zionist ideology; the farming lobby is a strong one in terms of domestic politics; and water is an emotional issue for the Israeli public. So far, the Israelis have sought to deflect attention away from the question of the sharing of existing water supplies by stressing the possibilities for increasing the amount of water available.

In all this, the Israelis' essential aim seems likely to be to ensure that any peace settlement guarantees them a minimum volume of water not less than present levels of consumption. If this is so, they will require that any peace treaty ensures their continued access to West Bank and Golan water, even if they agree to yield land for peace. In the case of the West Bank, the Israelis are unlikely to surrender enough water to permit any substantial development of irrigated agriculture there; and will probably insist on no change to the *status quo* during any transitional period of autonomy.

CONCLUSIONS

The demand for water in the Middle East will inevitably rise as a result of population growth and economic development. The consequence will be increased competition for water between the states within and bordering on the region. To secure their supplies, Middle Eastern states will resort to diplomatic pressure including trying to involve states outside the region, negotiation and attempts to block international funding of other states' projects.

As regards the Nile, Egypt has a breathing-space, mainly because of poverty and instability in upstream states. This will not last forever, but technical solutions may make more water available before those states are in a position to take significantly greater quantities of Nile water. In the Tigris–Euphrates basin, Iraq will have oil money which it can use to make up any shortfall in its food balance. The Syrians are in a less fortunate position, and may find their balance of payments deteriorating as they have to import food that they can no longer grow at home because of a reduced supply of water.

Until the beginning of the present peace process, the water issues in the Arab–Israel dispute must have seemed the most intractable water problems in the region. But the states sharing the water, and the Palestinians living under Israeli occupation, are now involved in (one might almost say locked into) a process which offers them a framework within which they can co-operate to deal with the crisis confronting them.

Finally, it is worth noting that water-sharing is not entirely a zero-sum game. There is the possibility of increasing the amount of water available: by tapping new aquifers, by bringing water from outside the region, and by greater use of desalination. What water is available can also be used more efficiently, notably through less wasteful methods of irrigation. Moreover, economic activity can be switched from agriculture to industry. All these steps involve effort and sacrifice, but ought to be more attractive for the states involved than going to war over water.

NOTES

1. Agreement for the Full Utilization of the Nile Waters, 1959.
2. Statement by Esam Radi, Minister of Public Works and Water Resources, *BBC Summary of World Broadcasts*, *SWB*, 17 May 1988.
3. There could also, however, be benefits: see, for example, the discussion in Guariso and Whittington, 1987.
4. Statement by Mohammed Tantawi, Minister of Defence, quoted by *Associated Press (AP)*, 19 October 1991.
5. Turkish Foreign Ministry spokesman, quoted by *AP*, 6 December 1989.
6. See, for example, *The Mideast Mirror*, 30 November 1993.

5. The regional economic impact of the Gulf War

Rodney Wilson

Sufficient time has elapsed since the Gulf War to judge its economic impact. In some respects it marked a turning point in Middle Eastern economic development, the end of one economic order, and the start of a new phase of development. At the political economy level there are some in the Middle East who see the outcome of the Gulf War, and the triumph of the forces of the great capitalist powers and their regional proxies, as a regional manifestation of the ending of the Cold War. Without this, and the Russian acquiescence in the West's efforts to defend its oil interests, the outcome might have been very different. In the changed post-Cold War circumstances it was possible for the United States to quickly build a regional alliance against Saddam Hussein to include not only the dependent regimes in the Gulf and Egypt, but also Syria, which hitherto had been within the Soviet orbit. It was the experience from this alliance building which was to provide the impetus for the subsequent breakthroughs in the Arab–Israeli peace process, which would not have been possible but for the hegemony of the United States in much of the region.

Some came willingly to the peace table, notably the Kingdom of Jordan, which has a long record of seizing opportunities from potentially disastrous situations. In many respects its record mirrors that of Israel. Others, notably the Palestine Liberation Organization, came reluctantly, largely because they had nowhere else to go, and their funding was running out. The Syrians came cautiously, knowing just how difficult it would be to secure the return of their territory, but nevertheless prepared to give peace a chance in the absence of any other solution. Only time will tell whether what may be in the end only a brief spell of Western hegemony will produce lasting results. This will ultimately depend to a considerable extent on whether the focus can be shifted to economic issues and away from the politics of power. Secularist socialism is certainly a spent force in the Arab world, and even before the defeat of Saddam the edifice of Ba'thism was crumbling in much of the region. Now even Saddam has been forced to see the realities of regional power by recognizing Kuwait.

Yet what might be seen as a Western triumph may contain the seeds of its own destruction. The Islamic parties see the secularist leaders in the region humbled and humiliated. The triumph of the Western order may have been pushed too far, and may provoke a backlash. Such an outcome is especially likely if the new externally imposed order does not result in an improved economic situation from which most in the region benefit. The omens are not encouraging. The PLO is being denied financial backing. Citizens in the Gulf are quite content to see their governments have declining real resources, as there is an unwillingness to part with private wealth to help the public purse of regimes whose intentions and allegiances are distrusted. Income tax remains politically unacceptable in the Gulf, and even charging the full price for utilities is resisted. Many are content to see their governments flounder, and get locked into Western dependency in the hope that this speeds their demise.

In Egypt and Algeria an alternative economic order has been created based on Islamic ideals in spite of official efforts to stop its spread, which include ruthless suppression. In Gaza the order is well established, with the PLO powerless to stop its further advance. This would not have been possible without the collapse of the nationalist and socialist alternatives to capitalism which the outcome of the Gulf War demonstrated. While their leaders court the West, and play the capitalist game, the masses are increasingly being influenced by the Islamic movement. Religious devotion has always been a fact of life in the Middle East. What is new is its renaissance in the economic and political sphere. For many the outcome of the Gulf War marked the end of any viable economic alternative to an Islamic order. It is against this background that the developments in the Middle East in the 1990s must be judged.

THE SIGNIFICANCE OF ECONOMIC FACTORS DURING THE PERIOD OF HEGEMONY

Most attention has been given to political developments since the Gulf War, especially the search for adequate regional security arrangements.

The Middle East peace talks represented a real breakthrough, especially for the Israelis and Jordanians, and to a lesser extent for the Palestinians, but it is clear that the discussion of substantive issues will be a long drawn-out affair. Perhaps inevitably there has been much less debate over economic matters, although it is taken for granted by all of the parties that any peace settlement would be accompanied by substantial financial assistance. Talk of a possible 'Marshall Plan' for the region may be unrealistic, especially as far as the Palestinians are concerned, but many believe that the United States was trying to send a positive signal by the partial debt relief for Egypt. The message was that co-operation would bring rewards. The deferment of assistance to Israel to cover the costs of resettling Russian Jews was also a deliberate attempt to show that the Bush administration could wield a stick as well as providing carrots, although Clinton has been much more unwilling to hold back finance for Israel.

If financial assistance is to make any contribution to economic development then there must be a favourable climate for growth. Unfortunately this is far from being the case where the poorer Arab countries are concerned. It is the existing rich countries of the Gulf which are in the most favourable position for further development. There has been some discussion of the need to redress the income inequality between the oil and non-oil states of the region, but it is by no means certain that external financial assistance will help contribute to this goal. At the same time substantial financial assistance from regional 'haves' to 'have-nots' seems less likely than in the past, especially as the Gulf states have become more inward-looking and have sought to cut themselves off to a considerable extent from the northern Arab countries.

Economic frustration was at the root of the conflict in the first place, as Saddam Hussein felt boxed in, unable to fund the reconstruction of his economy which had been shattered in the previous conflict with Iran. The oil rich states of the Arabian Peninsula were unwilling to provide financial help, and spent much time complaining about Iraq's inability to repay its previous debts. Only oil exports could provide the necessary revenue, but Iraq was unable to convince the other OPEC nations to allow an increase in its quota. At the same time over-production by neighbouring states such as Kuwait, which did not really need extra revenue, served to drive down world oil prices, and reduced even further the revenue Iraq could get from its limited exports.

For the state with the second largest oil reserves in the region, such a situation was intolerable. Saddam Hussein felt that if he did not take some action, his government, and perhaps even the Ba'th party, would have no future. Historically the oil fields of Saudi Arabia and Kuwait had been developed at Iraq's expense, as the rulers of these states had been more compliant with the interests of the multinational oil companies and the governments of the West. Resentments were deep-seated, especially as in many ways it was Iraq which was the more Westernized state, yet it had also been a victim of Western economic expediency which favoured the more conservative traditional regimes of the Arabian Peninsula.

ASSESSING THE SHORT-TERM ECONOMIC COSTS

The calculation of the financial cost of the Gulf War is a relatively straightforward matter conceptually, but in practice is much less simple. As far as the actual conflict was concerned, most of the cost was incurred by Iraq, with the losses in military equipment alone amounting to over $50 billion, though this figure is lower if the second-hand market value of the equipment is counted rather than the cost of purchase when new. Replacement rather than historical cost would, of course, be higher. The destruction of the Arab world's most expensive, and perhaps most sophisticated, military machine is only one aspect of the cost. The aerial bombardment of communications infrastructure inflicted damage of an equivalent amount, and the destruction of oil installations and industrial plant may have resulted in damage worth more than $130 billion.

Figures of this magnitude mean little in themselves, the real issue being the amount of time and effort needed to repair the damage and build replacement facilities. If there were no external constraints this would take about five years, although a military build-up to 1990 levels would take longer for Iraq. In practice, of course, the situation is more complicated, as there is the question of an arms embargo. As far as civilian reconstruction is concerned, the main worry is the reliance on imported supplies and the need to finance these. This can either be through increased oil revenues, although this is difficult while the prewar constraints remain, or through external financial assistance, although there is no obvious source for such.

For Kuwait the position is much easier, as although the Iraqis looted moveable property, the main infrastructure has remained intact, the most expensive damage being to oil installations. The industrial capacity of Kuwait was always limited, as government policy did not encourage local manufacturing because of labour shortages and a limited internal market. Instead oil revenues were recycled into international financial markets, and it is these investments which sustained the government-in-exile. As foreign assets worth over $70 billion remain, this should be more than adequate to finance the reconstruction required.

Saudi Arabia has also incurred costs due to the conflict, though physical damage was limited, given the ineffectiveness of the Scud missile attacks, the main destruction being to the small border town of Khafji and its refinery. The most costly damage was the environmental disaster caused by the oil slicks which cost more than $700 million to clean up. The much greater burden is that of contributing financially to the allied military effort for the defence of the Kingdom and the liberation of Kuwait. The bill for this exceeds $13.5 billion from the United States alone. There has been much publicity over the Saudi Arabian budget deficit and the borrowing of $3.6 billion from the Euro-market in London under an arrangement involving Morgan Guaranty.[1]

The cost of the war is, however, not a major problem for Saudi Arabia. The budget deficit of $6.7 billion has to be seen in the context of a gross domestic product of over $100 billion annually, and official overseas assets worth over $50 billion. Furthermore, there is no income tax, but such fiscal measures could easily be undertaken. In addition it has to be realized that Saudi Arabia increased its oil production by 50 per cent after the invasion of Kuwait and the imposition of economic sanctions on Iraq to make up for lost production from these countries. The revenue from this increased output has made an important contribution to reducing the costs incurred in hosting the allied forces and offering material support.

THE EFFECTS OF THE WAR ON OIL PRICES

After the invasion of Kuwait oil prices immediately rose from under $20 per barrel to over $30 per barrel in the spot market. Dealers were concerned that the invasion would prove a threat to oil supplies, which might affect not only Kuwaiti and Iraqi exports, but also those from Saudi Arabia, if Saddam Hussein's real aim was to be master of the Gulf oil fields and the dominant player in OPEC. With the strong response from the Bush administration, the diplomatic success of bringing together a formidable coalition against Baghdad and the passing of the United Nations Security Council Resolution 660, the markets regained some of their confidence, although there remained much uncertainty throughout the autumn and prices stayed well above pre-invasion levels.

The dispatch of United States and other allied forces to Saudi Arabia reassured oil dealers, as at least the Kingdom's huge supplies and reserves were no longer threatened by a leader challenging Western interests. The implementation of United Nations economic sanctions meant the informal ban on exports from Iraq and occupied Kuwait was formalized and implemented by most of the international community. This would have tended to increase oil prices had it not been for Saudi Arabia's policy of increasing exports to make up the shortfall. It was the uncertainty factor which caused prices to fluctuate in the $25 to $34 per barrel range, $9 to $18 over their average for the pre-invasion period. The premium itself reflected expectations about the future and worries about the effectiveness of the international response to the invasion, rather than actual supply shortfalls.

Once the deadline of 15 January 1991 was set for Iraqi withdrawal from Kuwait, oil dealers became more confident that there would be massive intervention which would guarantee oil supplies in the longer term. Oil prices fell, although it was not until the outbreak of the air war that they fell to their pre-invasion level, demonstrating that as far as oil dealers are concerned, actions speak louder than words. From then on even the worst of news was greeted calmly in the oil markets. Iraq's 'ecological terrorism' with the deliberate release of masses of oil into the Gulf to create giant slicks had little effect on oil prices. Even Saddam Hussein's 'scorched earth' policy with the destruction of Kuwait's well-heads and refining capacity did not unduly worry oil dealers. Once again it was long-term expectations that were to prove the crucial factor in oil-pricing, not immediate developments on the ground.

The effectiveness of the air war, and the very speedy and successful conclusion of the ground war, convinced those in the oil markets that price instability seemed much less likely in the years ahead. Western consumer interests would be more important in price determination, and Saudi Arabia's position as OPEC's swing producer was strengthened. The more populous oil-exporting states with limited reserves, such as Iran, had always favoured higher oil prices in the short term. Iraq, with its propensity for high military spending and need to reconstruct after the war with Iran, was in the same position. These interests were in conflict with those of the Western oil-importers. In contrast, there was no conflict as far as Saudi Arabia was concerned, as it has huge oil reserves and its main concern economically has been to keep prices low to ensure that Western consumers do not switch to alternative energy sources. If high prices did result in lower and diminishing demand, then in the end Saudi Arabia would be left with unsellable assets, rather like Britain's National Coal Board.

PALESTINIAN INCOME AND THE JORDANIAN ECONOMY

There can be little doubt that the Palestinians were not only political casualties of the Gulf War but also faced considerable economic damage. Before the war the Palestinians were by far the largest single immigrant group in Kuwait and many occupied well-paid positions. Their remittances were vital for the economies of the occupied territories and Jordan, and for every salary-earner in Kuwait there were several dependents left behind. Not only did the Palestine Liberation Organization (PLO) leadership support Saddam Hussein's position, but individual Palestinians informed on the Kuwaiti resistance, which resulted in torture and executions. Against this background, it seemed unlikely that any Jordanian passport-holders or those with Israeli identity documents from the West Bank or Gaza would be allowed back into Kuwait. In other Gulf states Palestinians also found themselves unwelcome. There have been some expulsions, and many work permits have not been renewed.

In addition to the loss of remittances, Jordan has been forced to purchase more expensive oil from Syria rather than obtain favourable barter terms from Iraq. This has added to Jordan's substantial trade deficit, as even before the Gulf War export receipts were less than one-quarter of import payments. Re-exports to Iraq virtually ceased even before the conflict, in spite of Jordanian reluctance to apply United Nations sanctions, severely reducing the country's external receipts.

Even without these difficulties the economic outlook for Jordan would have been dismal, as aid from Saudi Arabia fell in the mid-1980s following the oil price reductions at that time and, ironically, the need for Riyadh to assist Saddam Hussein financially in order to support the Iraqi position in the war with Iran. The ending of this earlier conflict and financial wrangling with Baghdad brought an end to this assistance in 1989, but there was no possibility of aid being re-routed to Jordan.

After the Gulf War this seemed completely out of the question given Gulf attitudes to King Hussein because of his stance over Baghdad.

In the past the Jordanian economy has proved to be remarkably resilient, recovering much faster than most outside observers expected from the 1967 war with Israel, the loss of the West Bank, and the civil war with the Palestinians (Wilson, 1991). External factors were extremely favourable, however, with inflows of aid and remittances after the 1973–74 oil price rises, and even high prices for phosphate, Jordan's major visible export. In the wake of the Gulf conflict the prospects for external assistance looked bleaker than ever as Jordan faced crisis yet again.

Living standards in Jordan have already fallen over recent years, and unemployment is an ever more serious problem. Even the educated, including university graduates, have been unable to find work. In the occupied territories the situation is much more desperate, however, as the failed uprising undermined the local Palestinian economy much more than the economy of Israel, where its effects have been marginal at best. The complete curfew during the Gulf War meant the population were prisoners in their own homes, and economic activity came to a standstill. Arab Palestinian workers have increasingly been replaced by the new flood of Jewish immigrants from the former Soviet Union. Such replacement began before the Gulf War, but was especially notable during the crisis and has continued in the period since. The resulting unemployment has become a permanent feature of the occupied territories, along with a very serious loss of income.

THE REGIONAL ECONOMIC BENEFICIARIES

In any conflict there are often economic as well as military winners and losers, and in a war over resources this is especially likely. As far as the Middle Eastern region is concerned, Egypt and Syria have appeared to be the main winners. Egypt clearly gained from the write-off by the United States of bilateral debts amounting to over $14 billion, which reduced its debt burden by a quarter virtually overnight. It of course lost some Suez Canal revenue and remittances before and during the conflict, but these were insignificant against this sum. Furthermore Egypt seemed set to play at least some role in the post-war Gulf, with its nationals replacing Palestinians in Saudi Arabia, Kuwait and elsewhere.

Figure 5.1   Middle Eastern trade: markets and deficits

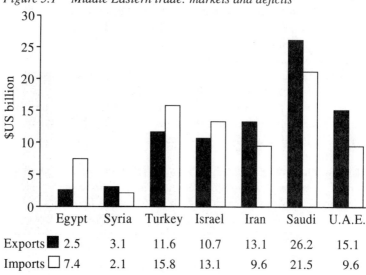

	Egypt	Syria	Turkey	Israel	Iran	Saudi	U.A.E.
Exports ■	2.5	3.1	11.6	10.7	13.1	26.2	15.1
Imports □	7.4	2.1	15.8	13.1	9.6	21.5	9.6

Source: World Bank Statistics, 1992.

Figure 5.2   High income Middle Eastern economies: gross national product per capita

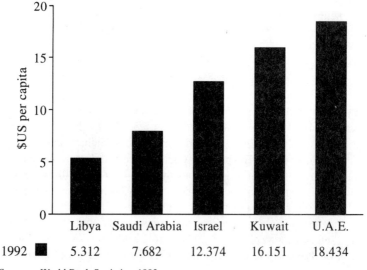

	Libya	Saudi Arabia	Israel	Kuwait	U.A.E.
1992 ■	5.312	7.682	12.374	16.151	18.434

Source: World Bank Statistics, 1992.

Figure 5.3   Middle income Middle Eastern economies: gross national product per capita

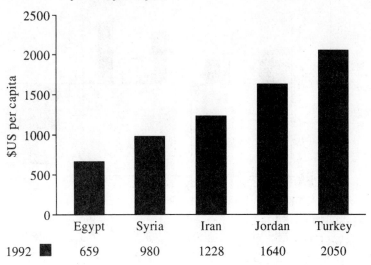

	Egypt	Syria	Iran	Jordan	Turkey
1992	659	980	1228	1640	2050

Source: World Bank Statistics, 1992.

Figure 5.4   Structure of production: sectoral shares of output

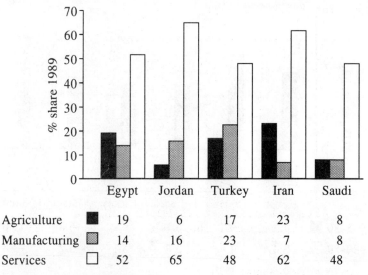

	Egypt	Jordan	Turkey	Iran	Saudi
Agriculture	19	6	17	23	8
Manufacturing	14	16	23	7	8
Services	52	65	48	62	48

Source: World Bank Statistics, 1992.

Figure 5.5   Consumption, investment and government: annual rates of growth or contraction, 1980–89

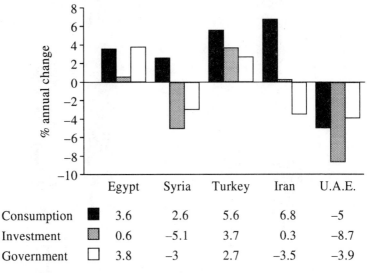

		Egypt	Syria	Turkey	Iran	U.A.E.
Consumption	■	3.6	2.6	5.6	6.8	−5
Investment	▨	0.6	−5.1	3.7	0.3	−8.7
Government	□	3.8	−3	2.7	−3.5	−3.9

Source: World Bank Statistics, 1992.

Figure 5.6   Economic growth in the Middle East: long term development trends

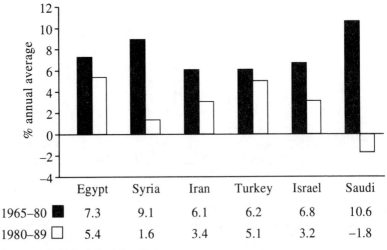

		Egypt	Syria	Iran	Turkey	Israel	Saudi
1965–80	■	7.3	9.1	6.1	6.2	6.8	10.6
1980–89	□	5.4	1.6	3.4	5.1	3.2	−1.8

Source: World Bank Statistics, 1992.

The economic gains from Gulf involvement are likely to be less than in the 1970s, however, as the states of the Arabian Peninsula can do much more for themselves in the 1990s, especially on the economic front. Recent Egyptian policy has nevertheless brought its rewards. Nasser fought a long and costly war in Yemen to acquire a military foothold on the Arabian Peninsula. Mubarak saw the Egyptian army playing a much more central role in Saudi Arabia, and has been paid to do so, though admittedly mostly by the United States.

Egypt has huge economic problems, with a population of 55 million to support, a very restricted cultivatable area, unviable state industries inherited from the Nasser period and a massive trade deficit. Sadat's 'open door' policy did not appear to be working, and economic reform was difficult. Price controls caused great distortions, and the phasing out of subsidies became an explosive political issue. There were endless disagreements with the IMF over economic policy, but negotiations had to succeed given Egypt's economic dependence. As always in Egypt, progress takes time, but Mubarak, to his credit, has quietly pursued the policies started by his predecessor, but with a greater understanding of what was needed in the economic sphere.

Development in Egypt will be a long haul nevertheless, as the challenges are enormous. The exchange rate system has been simplified and price distortions reduced, but basic structural problems remain, especially with the state-run industries. There has been talk of privatization, but few concrete measures, and manufacturing remains both domestically and internationally uncompetitive. Despite this, economic prospects for the post-Gulf War period appear better than they have been for over four decades, although the Mubarak regime continues to face domestic political uncertainties.

In the case of Syria the immediate economic benefits from its support are less tangible, but in the longer term these could be quite substantial. The Lebanese Christian militia leader, General Aoun, was one of the first casualties of the conflict, as he had been backed militarily by Iraq and had links with Tariq Aziz, Baghdad's Christian Foreign Minister. Aoun's demise removed a major source of friction and helped Syria consolidate its position in Lebanon with tacit Western approval. The collapse of the Soviet Union as a superpower and the state of the Russian economy were also of concern to President Asad, as his country's external economic and military relations had placed much emphasis on the Treaty of Friendship with the Soviet Union.

Syria has been wanting for some time to improve its relations with the West, and even before the Gulf conflict was rethinking and redesigning its economic policies. Its industrialization effort had been based on the establishment and development of state-owned plants and Soviet planning models. These had proved as unsuccessful in Syria as in the Soviet Union. Although in the 1970s it was usual to blame the state of hostility with Israel for the country's economic difficulties, by the 1980s it was recognized that a more realistic approach was needed.

In the late 1980s a series of new measures was enacted to encourage foreign investment and stimulate private sector activity. These had not really had time to work when the Gulf crisis erupted. In the post-Gulf War era, with Lebanon more stable and moves towards a new relationship between Damascus and the West, growing hopes emerged of economic recovery and improved living standards. Most Syrians have long tired of austerity and sacrifice for the sake of regional conflicts, and want to see a stronger domestic economy. The Asad government appears to have recognized this, and is rethinking its policies accordingly. This is perhaps one of the most promising changes in the region, from the point of view of future peace and stability.

REGIONAL INEQUALITIES AND DEVELOPMENT PROSPECTS

There has been considerable economic change in the Arab world in the last few decades, but the development process has been severely distorted. The countries of the region may have won a certain degree of political independence, at least from their former colonial powers, but economic independence has been illusory. The national boundaries inherited from the colonial era to some extent perpetuate wealth and income inequalities. The sparsely populated countries of the Arabian Peninsula have acquired substantial wealth because of their oil resources, but most surplus funds have been invested in the West, not recycled within the Arab world. There was little Arab solidarity before the Gulf War, but there has been even less since. Of course there are very different interpretations of the Arab economic predicament. The Arab Gulf countries assert that money invested in the northern Arab countries has largely been wasted, and there is considerable evidence to support this proposition. State-owned and state-run industries were established at huge expense in Egypt, Syria and Iraq, but none of the ventures has achieved commercial viability. Huge sums have been spent on military equipment, yet this has yielded no return in the conflict with Israel, and Iraq's humiliation demonstrates the futility of these efforts. There has been some agricultural improvement, but with rapid urban growth and increasing population pressures (even in rural areas), countries with substantial agricultural work-forces have become very dependent on food imports.

In contrast the Arab Gulf states have been much more successful in managing their funds. It is perhaps paradoxical that poor countries such as the Sudan have been unable to use their scarce resources effectively and have wasted meagre finances, while the Arab Gulf states have obtained good value for money. The recycled petro-dollars have brought ever more income, thanks to an intelligent investment policy in international financial markets. Kuwait throughout most of the 1980s earned more from its overseas assets than it did from oil. Saudi Arabia has built up the most modern petrochemical plants in the world, which are internationally competitive. The Kingdom has achieved not only self-sufficiency in grains, but even has an export surplus in wheat. Gulf Arabs used to be regarded by Iraqis and others as unsophisticated, lacking in education and know-how, and with the mentality of simple nomads. Yet they are now better educated than the Iraqis, and display greater technical skills and aptitudes. Far from being feudal economies, trapped in the past, it is the Arab Gulf states which lead the way economically in the region, while countries like Iraq have stagnated.

This growing economic imbalance was and remains a cause of instability. Envy and greed were important contributory factors to the Iraqi invasion of Kuwait. The former United States Secretary of State, James Baker, talked about addressing these imbalances of wealth and income, but it is hard to see how this could be done. The Arab Gulf states are likely to devote most of their efforts to helping each other, not the northern Arabs. Kuwait will be absorbed by its own reconstruction effort. Saudi Arabia may wish to devote more resources to strengthening its military forces as an insurance against further aggression.

The coalition may have scored an important military victory, but fostering a new regional economic order based on economic co-operation is likely to be more difficult than ever. The much quoted saying that 'winning the war may be much easier than winning the peace' does not only apply to the region's political conflicts, but also has economic and developmental implications. Four years after the Gulf War and almost two years since the mutual recognition by the PLO and Israel, the extent of the difficulty in externally imposing peace is apparent.

In the economic contribution to a volume on continuity and change in the Middle East, it would be tempting to see the change as being induced from outside, while the continuity is the reality from within, especially the continuity of Islamic values and culture. Such a view is simplistic however, certainly in the economic sphere. The communications revolution has also resulted in a dialogue between Muslims within and outside the region, and the development of new ideas in Islamic economics. The Gulf War highlighted the technical and military superiority of the West, but the peace process has illustrated its shortcomings in social and cultural understanding. It is in the realm of ideas that the battle will ultimately be won, yet it is here where Western concepts have been found wanting as far as the Middle East is concerned.

NOTE

1. *The Times*, 19 February 1991.

6. Iran: continuity and change since the revolution – carrying water in a sieve?

Christopher Rundle

INTRODUCTION

This chapter will focus on the dominant trend in Iranian foreign policy in the aftermath of the Gulf War, while looking also at the internal political background which brought that trend about.

Iran is clearly one of the countries which have been affected by the Gulf crisis of 1990–91. But it can be argued that what changes there have been recently are consistent with a trend in Iranian politics already evident at the end of the first 'Gulf conflict' – that is, the hostilities between Iran and Iraq which ended in 1988. This trend may be described as a trend towards pragmatism and towards a lessening in the ideological component in policy. Its origins can be traced back a long way, but it was the cease-fire with Iraq in 1988 and Khomeini's death in 1989 that enabled it to become the dominant trend. The Gulf crisis of 1990–91 gave further impetus to what was already there.

Even, of course, when there is a clear trend in Iranian politics, there are always people of significance pulling against it. In fact it has become a commonplace within Iran to talk about there being two political tendencies. As the elections to the fourth post-revolutionary Majles approached in April 1992 there was heightened activity by political groups supporting the government. There was also activity by others which, while supporting the Islamic Republic, wanted to reverse the prevailing trend. Naturally, groups which do not accept the Islamic Republic had no say in the matter.

An illustration of the way in which opposition to this trend has been expressed can be found in an article from a magazine published in Qom. The author contended that the values of modern diplomacy were incompatible with those of Islam; that the idea that a way could be found of preserving Khomeini's line without causing confrontation with the prevailing international norms was an insult to the revolution; and that those who imagined that it was possible to spread Islamic principles and values by means of conventional diplomacy were, in the words of the writer, attempting 'to carry water in a sieve'.[1]

It is also worth emphasizing that any attempt to divide Iranian personalities or groupings neatly into categories – extremists and moderates, radicals and conservatives, and so on – is bound to be an oversimplification. The factions function as loose coalitions of like-minded people, not as political parties with set membership or clearly defined policies. Individuals frequently have a foot in more than one camp, and often groupings come to be formed round a particular issue of the day, with their members having differing views on other issues. Moreover, we should bear in mind that those now labelled as pragmatists have been at the heart of the revolution since its beginning. They are believers, and have a pride in the revolution and its achievements.

IRANIAN POLITICS IN THE 1980S

Returning, however, to the prevailing dominant trend, it would not be fanciful to trace the effort towards reducing Iran's isolation back to the end of 1981. The principle began to emerge then of Iran being able to have relations with all states in the world except two or three – the two being Israel and South Africa and the third being the United States. In short, Israel was seen as illegitimate; South Africa as a racist country beyond the pale; and the US as being completely hostile to the revolution, though perhaps capable of one day 'changing its behaviour'.

It was at this time, after the fall of President Bani Sadr, that several of those now at the head of Iran's affairs achieved high office. Seyed Ali Khamene'i, now the leader of the Islamic revolution, became President in August 1981, and held that post until Khomeini's death. Ali Akbar Velayati, who had earlier been put forward by Khamene'i for the post of Prime Minister but failed to gain a vote of confidence, became Foreign Minister in December 1981; he still holds the post. Ali Akbar Hashemi Rafsanjani, now President of the Republic, was already Speaker of the Majles, as well as being one of Khomeini's most trusted lieutenants. There has been a high degree of continuity among the leadership since those days, little broken by Khomeini's death.

Another of those at the centre of things in those days was the Prime Minister, Mir Hossein Moussavi, who after the abolition of his post in 1989 became an adviser to Rafsanjani. Moussavi had, and has, a radical reputation. But in the last few months of 1981 one of his constant themes was the need for continuing, or even greater, contact with other countries. After a meeting with Khomeini in December 1981,[2] he gave an interview saying that if Iran's embassies abroad were closed this would please only those who were trying to isolate Iran – the US among them. Khamene'i, then President, spoke in similar vein in April 1982,[3] saying that it was in Iran's interest to develop its relations with its neighbours, and that Iran could have relations with West European, East European, African, Latin American and Asian countries, though it would not establish relations with the US unless the latter, as he put it, 'repented'. Nor, he added, would Iran establish relations with Israel. He was more expansive two years later, when he told a gathering of Iranian ambassadors that Iran should have an 'open-door' foreign policy, though this did not apply to those with which it definitely did not want to have relations at all.[4]

Whatever the theory, in practice Iran remained isolated in the mid-1980s, largely because of the continuation of the war with Iraq. Inside Iran this isolation bred a spirit of militancy which overshadowed all else; outside it caused fears of an eventual Iranian victory, and a leaning of many countries not directly involved in the conflict towards Iraq. Western attitudes were also affected by the American hostages episode, and by Iran's support for Hezbollah's activities in Lebanon. Khomeini must have felt at the time that there was ample evidence to justify his thesis that the world was divided into 'oppressors' (*mostakbarin*) and 'oppressed' (*mostazafin*).

Inside Iran, the period of the war saw the groups opposed to Khomeini's regime being eliminated, but also the emergence of clear divisions among those who followed his line. Factionalism continues, thereby reflecting the looseness of the coalition of opposition forces at the time of the revolution and the lack of a clear political programme on the part of the pro-Khomeini clergy who eventually became dominant.

At the time of the revolution it was possible to divide the groups active within it into three main categories: the extreme left-wing groups; the social-democrats; and the religious groups. The religious groups, which came to dominate, were extremely numerous, with names such as the Dawn of Islam, the Dawn of Hope, the Warriors of the Way of

Truth, the Muslim Community, and the Fedayeen of Islam. By far the most important organized group was the Islamic Republican Party (IRP). This was set up in February 1979 to provide an organized political structure for Khomeini's supporters. Its founders included Rafsanjani, Khamene'i and two more senior clerics, Beheshti and Bahonar, who were assassinated in 1981. Beheshti, who was head of the IRP, died along with many others when there was a massive explosion during a party meeting in June 1981. Bahonar was Prime Minister when he was killed in his own office building two months later – ironically at a meeting of government security officials.

The IRP soon became the dominant political party. In August 1979 a majority of the members of the Assembly set up to consider the draft constitution were either members of the party or associated with it. The struggle with President Bani Sadr in 1981 proved unequal because Bani Sadr had only a rudimentary political organization behind him – called the Office for Co-ordination of the People with the President – while the IRP, identified as his main opponent, had a vast clerical and revolutionary network at its disposal.

By 1983, with Khomeini's supporters triumphant, almost all the parties, whether of 'left' or 'right', had been driven underground, or abroad or both. Only the IRP's fortunes flourished. But once its opponents had been worsted it, too, was no longer needed: political management was being done by the clergy through other channels. Rafsanjani referred in 1984 to the existence of two trends within the party, and to consequent lack of decision. He wondered if a party with two such clear trends within it could survive. Three years later the party was dissolved. By then what had become important was the balance of power between the clerical factions within the pro-Khomeini coalition, not party politics as such.

Khomeini's own contribution to the debate was to talk about the 'Hezbollah' (literally 'the party of God') as the only party. This became part of a slogan: 'Only Hezbollah our party, only Ruhollah our leader'. Some people wondered if he intended that Iran should become a one-party state. But what he really meant was that the Islamic movement was the one valid political movement.

Another of Khomeini's contributions was that periodically he would knock together the heads of the competing factions. This meant that unity of a kind was maintained, but often at the expense of clarity in policy. His successor inherited a situation in which the factional struggle was not fully resolved.

The situation concerning political parties and groups since the death of Khomeini has been that – under legislation dating back several years – those which are licensed may function. But no mass party has been licensed; nor indeed has such a party applied for a licence. Some light was thrown on the leadership's attitude towards parties by an interview which President Rafsanjani gave in May 1991. Asked when the Political Parties Act would be implemented, he said that the Act had been communicated to the government and was being implemented.

> Evidently, [he said amid laughter from the audience] individuals do not dare form a party because they consider they will not succeed... If a party was going to be successful in Iran it was the Islamic Republican Party, which was endorsed by the Imam and all the ulema... The party could not establish itself as such and eventually it was extinguished. We are waiting for the emergence of parties, but they are not coming forward... .[5]

The so-called Political Parties Act had in fact four sections, dealing respectively with political parties and groups, Islamic societies, professional associations and religious minorities. This explains why those societies (rather than parties) which have been licensed are such a motley assortment. They include at least one from among the clergy but also groups such as the Association of Muslim Writers and Artists, the Islamic Women's Association, the Society of Surgeons and the Association of Paediatricians. Among the groups most recently licensed were the Welders Association and, interestingly enough, the Mojahedin of the Islamic Revolution, a pro-regime group which was very active immediately after the revolution (and which was broadly supportive of the IRP) but of which very little has been heard since.

Since the dissolution of the IRP two trends have continued to exist, both inside and outside the government, but with what is often described as the pragmatic trend growing in strength. At the time of the Majles elections in 1988 the two trends were identified with two clerical associations with almost identical names – the Militant Clerics Assembly of Mehdi Karroubi and Ali Akbar Mohtashami, and the Association of Militant Clergymen of Mohammad Reza Mahdavi-Kani. In Persian the distinction was between the *rowhaniyoun*, the radical faction, and the *rowhaniyat*, the more pragmatic faction. Neither had a clear-cut victory, and a large number of deputies were not allied with either faction, but the *youn* certainly had a significant representation. Moreover, after losing his post as Minister of the Interior, Mohtashami himself was elected to the Majles in a by-election the following year.

As previously noted, the pragmatic trend in Iranian politics was already in evidence when the war with Iraq was halted in 1988. This was a dramatic moment for Iran, with Khomeini likening the decision to 'drinking poison'. No full explanation was given at the time, though by making capital out of the shooting down of an Iran Air passenger aircraft by an American warship, and by referring to Iraq's use of chemical weapons, the Iranians sought to show that they were under pressure from a superpower and facing inhuman tactics. They also claimed that world peace was being threatened. Rafsanjani said that the full story would be told later.

The missing part of the story was provided in August 1991, when, in an interview with a Tehran newspaper, Rafsanjani commented:

> One of the factors in our accepting the cease-fire was one which we did not mention at the time and have not so far disclosed. It was a letter written by the Minister of Finance, and others responsible for economic affairs, which was discussed by the government and then submitted to the Imam; I as the military commander also studied it. They wrote that the country's economic and financial resources had reached the red light, and indeed had gone somewhat past the red light. They wrote that the situation was no longer tolerable for Iranian society... .[6]

The end of the war was thus, as many guessed at the time, caused by economic exhaustion as much as anything. War-weariness and a desire for a normal life have since been one of the principal factors in public support for the government's policies.

If ending the war was a supreme example of pragmatism, or expediency, coming to revolutionary Iran, there were others also to be found. The word 'expediency' is used because in February 1988 Khomeini set up a body called the 'Assembly for Determining the Expediency of the Regime' – the Expediency Council for short.

This was a body whose task was to resolve disputes between the Majles and the Guardian Council, the body which vets legislation from an Islamic and constitutional standpoint. The Majles and the Guardian Council had been at loggerheads over a number of issues, the underlying problem being that the Majles tended to favour reformist legislation whilst the wise men of the Guardian Council were more intent on safeguarding the purity of Islamic doctrine.

The creation of the Expediency Council and events leading to it sparked off a lively debate, though with Khomeini, of course, being the one voice of real authority. He explained his position in the following terms:

> The government, which is part of the absolute vice-regency of the Prophet, is one of the primary injunctions of Islam and has priority over other... injunctions, even prayers, fasting and the pilgrimage. The ruler is author-ized to demolish a mosque or a house which is in the path of a road and to compensate the owner for his house. The ruler can close down mosques if need be, or can even demolish a mosque which is causing harm... The government is empowered to revoke unilaterally any Islamic law agree-ments which it has concluded with the people when those agreements are contrary to the interests of the country or of Islam.[7]

The state's interests were thus being given priority over religious dogma, though of course the state, the Islamic Republic, was seen as acting in the ultimate interest of Islam.

Not long before his death in June 1989, Khomeini agreed to a review of Iran's constitution. This was completed soon after his death and enabled a more streamlined administration to be set up, with the post of Prime Minister being abolished and the President chairing the cabinet. The revised constitution also lowered the religious qualifications needed for becoming the leader of the Islamic revolution, allowing Khomeini to be succeeded by Khamene'i and in effect allowing for a greater degree of continuity in the leadership than would have been the case if one of the more senior religious figures had taken over.

These changes in attitude and institutions, together with the more relaxed international atmosphere after the end of the Iran–Iraq War, enabled Iran to give priority to the economy and to the rebuilding of ties with the outside world, particularly the West, which were necessary if it was to make a success of reconstruction. The process was held back by other aspects of Khomeini's legacy – particularly the Rushdie affair, which threatened to put everything into reverse. For a time the pragmatists had to tread very cautiously, and although there were no changes of personnel at the top, some shuffling of personnel within Iran's Ministry of Foreign Affairs and in embassies abroad took place in the aftermath of the decree. But the trend eventually reasserted itself.

IRANIAN FOREIGN RELATIONS SINCE 1988

A tone of increased pragmatism had also crept into foreign affairs in 1988, well before the ending of the war with Iraq. Rafsanjani went on record as saying that Iran had made too many enemies needlessly in the past, while a deputy foreign minister spoke of a new strategy of 'deepening and developing' relations with the countries of the European Community.

Notable events in the year between Khomeini's death and Iraq's invasion of Kuwait included the Azerbaijan crisis in the Soviet Union in early 1990 and the earthquake in north-west Iran in June of that year. In the former instance, Iran's new government passed its first foreign policy test by acting in a restrained manner and was not tempted to be drawn in on the side of fellow Muslims. In the latter instance, the need for international assistance for the earthquake victims was undeniable, and extreme voices raised in Tehran against it were easily quelled.

The Gulf crisis of 1990–91 produced an immediate benefit for Iran in that it led to progress in implementing UN Security Council Resolution 598, the Resolution ending the Iran–Iraq War. Since 1988 a cease-fire had been in place but no progress had been made in implementing the rest of the Resolution. Iraq now wished to neutralize its eastern border and redeploy its troops. It therefore decided in August 1990 to withdraw from Iranian territory and begin an exchange of prisoners-of-war. In correspondence with President Rafsanjani, President Saddam Hussein also agreed in principle to return to the 1975 Algiers agreement. The Iranians hailed this as a major political victory.

Iraq's defeat by the international coalition and the cutting down to size of its military capability were clearly to Iran's advantage. Iran gained international credit by supporting United Nations resolutions and by being non-belligerent, despite a call by Ayatollah Khalkhali to take up arms against the US. It used the opportunity to rebuild its own bridges with the UN and with individual members of the international community. Since August 1990 diplomatic relations have been re-established with the United Kingdom, Saudi Arabia, Jordan, Morocco and other countries, and an interests section has been opened in Egypt. Existing relations with a number of countries have been upgraded to ambassadorial level.

The UN Secretary-General's report in December 1991, blaming Iraq for the start of the Iran–Iraq conflict, was hailed as another victory, even though Iran's aim of turning that to its financial advantage through gaining reparations from Iraq or some kind of assistance from other Arab states could not be certain of success. Rafsanjani said the report was the delayed result of the sacrifices of Iranian combatants over a period of years. The *Iranian News Agency* (*IRNA*) went as far as to say that, 'the ruling of the UN is also flying colours for the Islamic Republic of Iran and its foreign policy planning'.[8] Certainly such comment reflected a marked improvement in relations between Iran and the UN, which had not been good since the revolution.

The process of normalizing relations with other countries has not, however, been trouble-free. Relations with Egypt provided an example of conflicting trends at work. Barely had the two countries moved to patch up their relations a little when the Madrid conference took place, Iran held its own Palestinian conference, and Egypt's attitude to Israel was being publicly denounced in the Majles. Suggestions by the head of the Majles's Foreign Affairs Committee that Iran should develop its relations with Egypt, South Africa and Morocco, led to fierce argument. Relations with Morocco were in fact soon resumed, but at that stage there was no immediate prospect of a resumption of relations with Egypt.

If Iran came out of the Gulf crisis with a number of foreign policy successes, there were negative aspects also. Not only has Saddam Hussein survived – so far at any rate – but American power and prestige in the region have been strengthened. Much of what Iran is now doing in the area seems conditioned by this. Iran would like to see the Arab–Israel peace talks fail, for fear that they would lead to still greater US influence; hence what seems to be increased attention to Palestinian affairs in Tehran. In the Persian Gulf Iran has long advocated security arrangements by the local countries themselves, and argues that since it has the longest coastline in the Gulf it would make no sense to exclude it from regional arrangements. It is opposed to bilateral agreements between regional states and outside powers of the kind entered into by Kuwait and the United States, and has criticized the memorandum of understanding between Kuwait and the United Kingdom. Iran is also sensitive to American policy towards the former Soviet republics, and concerned at the prospect of co-operation between Turkey and the US in that area. The Tehran press has gone so far as to suggest that the US is seeking to create there, with Turkey's assistance, a new bloc based on ethnic divisions.

The new situation in Central Asia provides for Iran both opportunities and hazards. The main hazard is that ethnic unrest may spill over the border, particularly in Azerbaijan. A note of warning was struck in December 1991 by a Tehran newspaper: 'The unstable conditions in those republics could be the cause of serious insecurity along the lengthy borders (over 2,000 km) which Iran shares with those countries'.[9]

The threat to Iran's integrity should not be exaggerated, but it does have a legitimate concern and it may not be easy for Tehran to manage the new situation and balance its various objectives. For example, while cultivating relations with Azerbaijan it wants to stay on good terms with Armenia because of the substantial Armenian community in Iran, many of whose members are businessmen and artisans who contribute to the Iranian economy. Velayati's attempt to mediate between the two sides in the Nagorno–Karabakh dispute was evidently undertaken out of real concern that the conflict was intensifying. One of the fears which is not usually highlighted is that Iran does not want another major influx of refugees to add to the three million or so Afghans, Kurds and others to which it is already playing host.

On the plus side for Iran, economic opportunities are presenting themselves, as well as new opportunities to develop cultural influence. Typically, the Iranian government has been treading quite cautiously, but it has been active, among other things, in establishing new diplomatic relations. Iran has upgraded its consulate-general in Baku (Azerbaijan) to an embassy and has opened new embassies in Turkmenistan, Tajikistan and Kazakhstan. Although it was behind Turkey in recognizing Azerbaijan, it was the first foreign country to open an embassy in Tajikistan. An Iranian deputy minister said at the time that the expansion of ties between Iran and Tajikistan was, 'a natural continuation of common history between the two nations which was disrupted during 70 years of communist rule'.[10]

It is debatable whether Iran will most easily develop ties with Azerbaijan, where there is a common border and the population are predominantly Shia Muslims; with Turkmenistan, which also has a common border and perhaps the greatest need for economic co-operation; or with Tajikistan, which shares with Iran a common language. Cultural ties – those of language, literature and music – may in fact prove stronger than any; one example of co-operation in this sphere came in January 1992 when Iran agreed to help Tajikistan print school books in Persian for students, following a decision to switch the Tajik script from Cyrillic to Persian. Iran is also training Tajik diplomats. Ties with Kazakhstan and Kirgizstan, however, are less well developed.

Iran obviously sees scope for expanding economic and commercial ties in the area. As *IRNA* has put it: 'The disintegration of the Soviet Union into independent republics has brought into sharper focus the important geo-political situation of the Islamic republic as the bridge between landlocked Central Asia and the outside world...'.[11]

The Iranian provinces are now all geared up to expand border trade and passenger traffic with their new-found neighbours.

From the perspective of some of the republics, particularly Turkmenistan, shorter routes to the oceans via the Gulf than are available via the Russian railways to the Black Sea and the Baltic must be attractive, and a visiting British Member of Parliament recently claimed to have detected 'a gleam in the eye' of an Iranian official when he spoke of the desire of the Muslim republics to find alternatives to the Russian rail network.

By mid-February 1992 Foreign Minister Velayati was able to say that Iran had signed more than a hundred agreements with the republics. With regard to the development of new economic relationships, the Caspian littoral countries, namely Iran, Russia, Azerbaijan, Kazakhstan and Turkmenistan, have demonstrated a desire to co-operate in shipping, joint oil and gas exploration and fisheries, and in February 1992 announced they were forming a new Caspian grouping. Talks have been held about the future of the natural gas pipeline from Iran to the former Soviet Union. Turkmenistan has said that it will switch its oil purchases from Russia to Iran. Five of the newly independent republics were admitted to membership of the Economic Co-operation Organization (ECO), initially comprising Iran, Pakistan and Turkey, at a summit meeting in Tehran in February. Kazakhstan attended as an observer. Iran has said that it favours creating an even larger Islamic common market, which might include Afghanistan when a settlement is eventually reached there.

There are conflicting perceptions of Iranian activities in Central Asia. One is quite prevalent in the West, and is to be found also in some of the Arab countries. This sees the spread of Iranian influence as a threat to regional stability because of the potential for 'exporting the revolution'. Another is provided by the Iranians themselves, who see it as natural that they should develop relations with the neighbouring, newly independent republics, and that, just as Christianity has begun to flourish again in Eastern Europe and Russia, Islam should flourish again in parts of the former Soviet Union inhabited by Muslims. They also say that one of the motives for expanding the ECO was its perceived potential contribution to peace and stability in the area, allowing mutual confidence among the various states to develop. One of the questions this raises must be whether the ECO will be able to transcend rivalries between Iran and Turkey in particular.

CONCLUSION

Iran is evolving in a direction which has been clearly signalled since 1988. One can even see some continuity in thought since as far back as late 1981. There is also some continuity between pre-revolutionary and post-revolutionary policies. The Shah believed in good-neighbourliness and in making Iran the dominant power in the Gulf. The present government subscribes to similar principles, though its advocacy of the first is weakened by its Islamic revolutionary ideology, and the second can at present be only an ambition: it will be years before Iran has made good the military and economic losses sustained in the hostilities with Iraq.

Iran is now putting increased emphasis on the practical interests of the state. A more cautious approach is being developed towards international affairs. President Rafsanjani's comments on this subject appear to confirm this view:

> The Islamic Republic of Iran has passed through the special stage of consolidation and defence and now, in the new world conditions, must consolidate itself further and take its place in the world through a different perspective... By working in a subtle way and using appropriate means, we can advance on the world stage... We need a prudent policy, both for inside the country, in order to strengthen our base, and for our foreign policy... We have no need to speak fanatically. We have no need to chant impractical slogans.[12]

That is certainly a far cry from 1979.

The problem of 'carrying water in a sieve' is nevertheless there. If ideological principles may be tainted by contact with the outside world, as feared by some in Qom, so may state policy be knocked off course by Islamic revolutionary considerations. Iranian leaders no doubt recognize the problem. The question is how they will handle in future the sometimes conflicting demands of the two tendencies.

NOTES

1. *Pasdar-e-Eslam*, No. 119, 1991–2, p. 38 (writer's name was not published).
2. Press interview, 6 December 1981.
3. Press interview, 6 April 1982.
4. *Iranian News Agency (IRNA)* report, 6 August 1984.
5. News conference, Tehran, 5 May 1991 reported in *BBC Summary of World Broadcasts (SWB)* ME/1065, 7 May 1991.

6. *Ettela'at*, 9 August 1991.
7. *SWB* ME/0043, 8 January 1988.
8. *IRNA* report, 11 December 1991.
9. *Tehran Times*, 30 December 1991.
10. *IRNA*, Tehran, 12 January 1992.
11. *IRNA*, Tehran, 9 January 1992.
12. Speech by Rafsanjani, 20 December 1991.

7. The continuity of Russian and Soviet policy in the Middle East

Derek Hopwood

INTRODUCTION

In 1552 the forces of Ivan the Terrible, ruler of Moscow and Kiev, occupied the city of Kazan, capital of Tatarstan. This event inaugurated several centuries of Russian imperial expansion. In March 1992 the people of the autonomous republic of Tatarstan voted in a referendum for independence from the Russian Federation. This vote fittingly symbolized the breakup of the Russian–Soviet Empire and in a way brought Russian history full circle. The long period of expansion was over. For a few years under President Gorbachev the Soviet Union had tried to act as a superpower with a communist ideology but the withdrawal from Afghanistan was an admission that the old, aggressive, expansionist communist state could no longer function. The fall of Gorbachev and the end of communism was a watershed as great as, if not greater than, the Bolshevik revolution of 1917.

The continuity of Russian–Soviet policy in the Middle East had been interrupted, possibly never to be resumed. The disappearance of the Soviet Union meant the end of a Soviet policy which was itself a continuation of old Tsarist aims. The future can only be uncertain. The new Russia is not a superpower seeking to dominate the world and the former Soviet republics will certainly wish to conduct individual foreign policies.

It is informative to read recent comments of Soviet and Russian officials on foreign policy which display a mixture of regret and frankness. There is little idea of future aims, severe criticism of past activities and frank assessment of failures and mistakes. The Russian intelligentsia's traditional inferiority complex has burst to the surface and self-abasement is in vogue.

This author's first research in the Middle Eastern field was a study of Russian policy in Syria and Palestine from 1843 to 1914 (Hopwood, 1969). It traced the growth of Tsarist interests in the area, of Russian relations with the Ottoman Empire and the ideological background to the expansion of the Tsarist Empire. This led on to a consideration of the continuity of Russian–Soviet interests in the Middle East and to the conclusion – *mutatis mutandis* – that Soviet activity was largely a continuation of Russian policy in the 19th century. The Bolshevik revolution of 1917 was a watershed, but Russia continued to exist as a state and as an Empire. The Russian historical memory and experience could not be erased and Russian methods and aims did not change overnight. A historical approach could perhaps help to explain Soviet policy, and put both the Cold War and the dramatic collapse of the Soviet Empire into perspective. Soviet Middle Eastern policy has come to an end and the history of Russian–Soviet imperial expansion is a finite subject.

Great power rivalry was a major theme of the history of the Middle East from the 18th until the mid-19th century. During this period Britain and France were the main rivals of Russia. For some 40 years after the Second World War the world lived in the era of superpower rivalry when America and the Soviet Union became the chief protagonists, with China on the sidelines. At the end of the Cold War, with the European Community playing a secondary role, the United States was left unchallenged. While the consequences of the new global power configuration are unforeseeable, the Gulf War would not have taken place in the same way if the Soviet Union had still been influential in the area.

Russia in the beginning was a land power based, in the 15th and 16th centuries, on Kiev and Moscow. The taking of Kazan in 1552 started a long process of expansion in all directions. This implanted something in the Russian soul, a search for new frontiers, a restless longing to move into new and remote areas. The frontier mentality was part of Russian history and literature, and dissidents could always be exiled into the remotest of areas. In addition, all kinds of other peoples were slowly absorbed into Mother Russia adding to the variety and ethnic mix of the country. Tatars, Bashkirs, Turks, Poles, Kazakhs and many others were annexed. Territorially, the expansion reached the Baltic in 1700 when Tsar Peter the Great opened his window to the west in St Petersburg, a cold-water port which was frozen over in winter.

To the north, Russia expanded into the limits of Siberia. In the late 18th century Russia, under Catherine the Great, moved southwards through Cossack territory to reach the Black Sea. This provided a warm-water port but access to the Mediterranean was guarded by the Ottoman Empire seated in Constantinople on the Straits of the Bosporus. Russia felt trapped by this fact and had tried to dominate or even dismantle the Ottoman Empire. Catherine had conceived a great plan, her Oriental project, by which the rival Empire would be partitioned. Grand Duke Constantine, the second son of the heir-apparent, was brought up in the Greek tradition and the plan was to place him on the throne of a revived Byzantine Empire. Russia fomented rebellion in the Crimea, the Morea and Georgia and this provoked Turkey to declare war in 1769. The Russian fleet entered the Mediterranean and landed troops in Greece and Lebanon. In Europe the Ottoman armies were overwhelmingly defeated and Turkey was compelled to sign the Treaty of Küçuk Kaynarca in 1774. Considering that the Ottoman armies had everywhere been defeated and that Russia had occupied the Crimea, Wallachia, Moldavia, Bessarabia and Georgia, the terms of the treaty were moderate. The Crimea and Bessarabia were given independence and the other lost territories were restored to Turkey. There was no rebirth of the Byzantine Empire and no new emperor in Constantinople, but it did mean that the Black Sea became a Russo-Ottoman lake and the treaty assured Russian commercial vessels unrestricted navigation there and through the Bosporus Straits. It did not, however, lessen Russian ambitions ultimately to gain full control of Constantinople and the Straits themselves.

Soon after, the Ottoman Empire was powerless to prevent the subsequent annexation of the Crimea by Russia in 1783 – the first loss in modern times of a purely Muslim area to a Christian power. War was once again declared in 1787 but a British threat to support Turkey against a Russian invasion led Catherine to sign the Treaty of Jassy by which territorial acquisitions west of the Dnester were renounced and thoughts of freeing Greece and Constantinople from the Turks were temporarily abandoned.

Catherine's successor, Tsar Paul, sought and secured a friendly understanding with Turkey hoping to extend Russian influence to the shores of the Mediterranean by diplomacy rather than by force of arms. In fact after 1825, on the death of Tsar Alexander I, Russia abandoned the goal of conquering Constantinople in favour of keeping Turkey a weak and dependent power.

Elsewhere, by the early 19th century Russia was moving forward in Transcaucasia, now acquiring the ancient kingdoms of both Georgia and Armenia and gaining recognition of these conquests by Turkey and Persia. In Central Asia, Russian territory extended to the frontiers of Persia and Afghanistan when it absorbed further independent Muslim states: Samarkand in 1868, Bukhara in 1873, Tashkent in 1884 – all of which have now reclaimed independence. In the Far East the Pacific was reached when Vladivostok, 'possessor of the East', was founded in 1860.

Thus Tsarist Russia had reached the limit of expansion: an Empire extending 7,000 miles from west to east and incorporating many peoples. In the north and east geography was the limiting factor; elsewhere other states imposed barriers. However, empires ceaselessly need to protect themselves with further frontier areas, and the Russian Empire was no exception. As it sought secure frontiers Russia looked for new areas of expansion to protect its new acquisitions. But in the Middle East the other powers, Britain, France, Turkey and Austria, resisted new movements once the borders of Persia, Afghanistan and certain parts of the Ottoman Empire had been reached.

During the 19th century Russia pursued certain foreign policy aims. Count Lamzdorf, one of its Foreign Ministers, claimed that Russian policy was, 'first of all an Asiatic policy'. While this was undoubtedly an exaggeration, and Russia was also clearly concerned with its relations with Europe despite the absence of war there for a century (apart from that in the Crimea), its policy towards the Ottoman Empire was often of prime importance. In general, the aim of Tsarist Russia was to be recognized as being equal to the other European powers in determining the future of the Ottoman Empire, as a power to be consulted, and to be regarded as a 'great power'. This implied that Russia had to accept a responsible role in the balance of power even when asserting its own claims. It was a system based on self-interest and to some extent on the belief that a balance preserved was better than a state of instability, rivalry and war. Of course the system often failed, especially when one power attempted to dominate another. The Napoleonic invasion and the blockade in the 19th century had engendered a sense of insecurity and a fear of encirclement in Russia. Consequently it was fearful of any alliance or power which seemed to threaten its security.

The Ottoman Empire, Russia's largest neighbour in the Middle East, was weakening in the 19th century watched anxiously by Europe. Russia wanted to keep it a weak dependent power, although was not averse to nibbling off pieces of Ottoman territory if possible. And, as one Foreign Minister, Nesselrode, wrote in 1829: 'If Providence willed the fall of the Ottoman Empire then Russia would bow to the inevitable'. One of Russia's chief aims was to obtain free passage for its warships from the Black Sea into the Mediterranean through the Straits of the Bosporus. Britain felt this would upset the balance of power and, by the London Convention of 1841, the great powers insisted that Turkey forbade passage of any foreign warships, including those of Russia, in times of peace.[1] Britain did not want the growth of a strong Russian fleet in the Mediterranean which could threaten the British position in Egypt or the passage of ships through the Suez Canal to India. Russia, on the other hand, was always pressing for free passage and access to warm-water ports. The Straits were also important as a trade route for Russian exports and for a passenger line to the Near East.

In addition to its strategic and diplomatic interests in Constantinople, Russia had deep religious concerns. It claimed that on the destruction of Byzantium by the Turks, leadership of the Christian Orthodox world had passed to Moscow, the third Rome. Russia further claimed that as a result it had assumed responsibility for all the Orthodox Christians in the Ottoman Empire, whether in Syria and Palestine, Greece, the Balkans or in Turkey itself. It thus considered itself spokesman and defender of these Ottoman subjects, and if it felt that either its prestige or their welfare were at stake it was prepared to go to war.

This fellow feeling for Orthodox Christians, or pan-Orthodoxy, intertwined with another current of thought, namely pan-Slavism, which could be taken as the ideology of imperial Russia. It was a mix of devotion to Mother Russia and the Church, a messianic urge to spread Russian Orthodox culture, and a militancy which sought to unite all Slavs under Russian hegemony. It was an ideology strongly embraced by some men who had responsibility for Russia's foreign policy. In order to unite all Slavs, many of them would first have to be 'liberated' from the Ottoman yoke. This aim was extended to include subjects who were not Slavs but who were, nevertheless, Orthodox Christians: notably Greeks and Arabs. Some Russians set their sights on the creation of a great Orthodox empire which would include Jerusalem, Palestine and Constantinople. Catherine the Great had had such dreams, but any attempt to put such a policy into practice in the 19th century would have been strongly opposed not only by Turkey but also by other European powers. But this dream, this messianic all-embracing solution, was not untypically Russian, and even if it could not be achieved immediately it could rest in the minds of the dreamers as a long-term ambition.

In pursuing its foreign policy Russia utilized those methods favoured by all great powers. It is important to remember, however, that it is difficult to find any great consistency or even perseverence in pursuing long-term aims. Consistency was hindered by frequent changes of personnel, interdepartmental rivalries, conflicting ideologies and personal quarrels.

First, Russia made policy by issuing threats against other powers which might lead to war. It made demands for greater privileges in passage through the Straits, or for greater influence in Ottoman internal affairs which on two notable occasions led to major wars: the Crimean in 1854 and the Russo-Turkish of 1876. Whenever its demands were rejected or its armies defeated it had to fall back on negotiation or conference, when it usually had to admit that as a partner in the balance of power it could not step too far out of line, particularly if faced with a united reaction on the part of other powers. At the Conference of Berlin Russia was compelled to disgorge certain of its territorial gains, and the Crimean War was fought to resist its claim to a preponderant influence in the Ottoman Empire. When thus blocked it might turn its attention to other areas of Asia. Britain tried persistently to keep a check on further Russian expansion, in Afghanistan, Persia or the Gulf. As Lord Curzon made clear: 'A single Rusian port in the Persian Gulf would constitute a wanton rupture of the *status quo*'.

Great powers traditionally attempt to gain access to, and influence in, an area outside their national territory by patronizing local clients, who together may constitute a whole nation, a party or sect of similar beliefs or ideology. The power offers the 'benefits' of protection, financial aid, training and education to its clients, but these can be dropped if circumstances change or if the interests of the power so demand. A power will always put its own interests before those of its clients; its relations with other powers are the more important. In the Ottoman Empire Russia became the protector of, and spokesman for, the Slavs and the Orthodox Christians: Greeks, Bulgarians and Arabs. In Palestine and Syria many of the religious or ethnic groups were adopted by one or other of the powers: Russia played for the Orthodox Arab community. It built for them schools, hospitals and churches, offered financial aid, education locally and in Russia, and interfered with the national movement developing among the Orthodox Arabs at the close of the 19th century. But the attentions of an outside power are not always welcome to the recipients and not all Orthodox Arabs wanted to become clients or protegés of Russia.

In 1914 Russian activities in the Middle East were brought to a halt. Once again it found itself fighting against Turkey. Russia had had certain successes and certain failures in the area up to the outbreak of war. It had gained recognition as a great power in the Middle East and, during allied negotiations in 1916, on the future of a defeated Ottoman Empire it was promised possession of Constantinople and the Straits. During the fighting Russian troops advanced as far as the outskirts of Baghdad. At certain periods during the 19th century other powers feared that a Russian seizure of Jerusalem was planned and imminent. It had established a certain presence in Palestine and Syria. Its schools and churches were visible symbols of Russian prestige and concern and many Orthodox Christians looked to the Tsar as their protector. But unlike Britain and France, Russia had gained no Arab territories. The Suez Canal remained in British hands, the Straits remained closed to Russian warships, and further Russian expansion was blocked. Russian cultural influence was minimal as Russian was not considered to be a useful language, and an education in France was much preferred by many Syrians and Egyptians.

The Bolshevik revolution of 1917 swept away the organizations and institutions through which Russia had pursued its policies in the Middle East. Great changes took place in Russia itself and initially great changes were expected by the communists in other parts of the world, although these expectations were soon dashed. The communist revolution was not exported and the new Soviet leaders had to come to terms with the political world in which they lived: a world of compromise where ideology had often to be subordinated to practical demands. But beside or beneath a more realistic assessment of the possibilities of foreign policy there persisted the belief in the historical inevitability of the triumph of communism, however distant the triumph might be. This feeling was surely a continuation of the 19th century belief in the messianic mission of Russia to conquer and convert the world.

Soviet Russia had inherited the mantle of a great power in the mould of the Tsarist Empire; none of the conquered territories was given up and the reins of power remained centrally in Russian hands, although now in Moscow rather than St Petersburg. The Soviet Union was still a large empire with the mentality that the maintenance of such an institution seems to demand. Its aims remained basically those of the previous regime and the policies followed exhibited, *mutatis mutandis*, similar features. A great power demands a right to pursue a policy in all parts of the world, to be consulted on world problems, and the Soviet Union specifically sought to counter-balance the world-wide influence of the United States. The Soviet Union conducted a 'total policy' making no distinction between diplomatic, economic, psychological or even military means of operation, nor did it make any fundamental distinction between domestic and foreign policy. Policy decisions were made at the highest level in the Soviet Politburo and foreign policy decisions were not handled specifically by the Foreign Ministry. Soviet policy was essentially active and militant, probing, seeking out opportunities, ready to take advantage of signs of weakness or lack of resolve in others. It was a difficult mode of policy for Western powers to combat.

Soviet leaders would have explained their policy in at least two ways. First, it was part of the inevitable progress towards a communist universe which was to be speeded up with Soviet help. Secondly, it was, with regard to the United States, a 'compensatory' policy, namely an attempt to equal or excel the United States in all fields. From the historical perspective, the Soviet Union was trying to catch up with America and attain at least a balance in world affairs. One aspect of this policy, applying specifically to naval matters but characteristic of much more, was firmly underlined by a Soviet admiral: 'The time when Russia could be kept out of the world's oceans has gone for ever. We will sail all the world's seas. No force on earth can prevent us'.[2] From the historical perspective this statement reveals echoes of the Napoleonic blockade of Russia and of the Russo-Japanese War.

From the Soviet point of view it was intolerable that the US navy should dominate the Mediterranean. No one navy, as earlier the Royal Navy had done, could demand an exclusive presence in any one area. The difference between Soviet and American policy was that the United States pursued a more open policy of professed peace-keeping while Soviet policy was secret and therefore mysterious and potentially dangerous. But on occasions it seemed that the Soviet Union was learning one of the lessons of being a great power, and ultimately a superpower, in that the exercise of power brought responsibilities as well. There were areas in which the interests of the other had to be taken into account.

A concomitant of being both a great power and a communist state was the need for territorial expansion, a continuation of 19th century policy. Expansion had to take place wherever and whenever possible and, even more importantly, all territory under Soviet or communist rule had to remain so. This was explained both by the necessity for the continued advance of communism and by the history of the expanding Russian state. Stalin looked to expand frontiers in all directions. If new territory could not be annexed or dominated then at least no adjoining state could be allowed to threaten Soviet security. Moscow considered the maintenance of peace and security in territories bordering the Soviet Union to be in the Soviet people's vital interest. The Soviet Union thus continued to be an imperial power in the true 19th century sense. It controlled the old Tsarist Empire and continued to try to export Soviet (Russian) communist culture to less fortunate peoples.

The obverse side of the coin of a constant Soviet advance was the attempt to contain other powers and alliances. The Soviet Union attempted actively to oppose all Western efforts to penetrate and influence other countries. It opposed the NATO–CENTO–SEATO grouping which smacked far too much of a threat of encirclement. The Straits had to be kept open to all types of Soviet shipping; ports and bases were sought as were outlets for free trade. Any movement which was ostensibly opposed to Western influence could have claimed Soviet support.

Whilst the Soviet Union was attempting to pursue a great power policy, the role of ideology was not always beneficial. Just as the pan-Slav–Orthodox ideology influenced Tsarist policy, communism was, at least theoretically, the motivating factor behind Soviet activities. In practice, however, the Soviet Union dealt with non-communist regimes in which members of the local communist party were often imprisoned and which followed bourgeois nationalist policies. Soviet politicians had to deal with such countries while the idealogues closed their eyes or claimed that the countries were progressive, anti-imperialist and, at least, on the road to socialism.

The methods used by the Soviet Union in its policy were largely the same as those employed by imperial Russia. It made threats, used force, backed warring parties and tried negotiation if coercion failed. At the same time there was endless criticism of the actions of others not considered to be in the same camp, particularly of the United States. The Soviets also made the attempt to adopt clients in the Middle East, those who could become dependent on them for aid and arms, education and training. This policy had its problems in the then nationalist atmosphere of the 'Third World', as no state which had recently thrown off the shackles of a colonialist regime wished to become beholden to another power. There was much talk about non-alignment and a naive assumption that the Soviet Union was disinterested in backing so-called non-aligned countries. The Soviets on occasions adopted 'unreli-able' clients who accepted aid, but did not want a strong Soviet pres-ence and even expelled Soviet experts and advisers. Nevertheless, the Soviet Union continued to build up its presence in the Middle East, through its navy, base facilities and prestige projects. If in the 19th century the symbol of Russian power and prestige was the Russian Orthodox cathedral in Jerusalem, in the 20th century it was the Aswan High Dam. Finally the Soviet Union attempted to build links with local communist parties, but with little success. The parties were too small and weak, there was a weak working class basis and the ideas of Arab nationalism had a stronger appeal than those of international commu-nism. Even the Arab parties which did exist were wary of being tied too closely to the USSR.

Until the Second World War both Lenin and Stalin had tried to bully and to make demands on neighbouring states. The Soviets had by then concluded non-aggression pacts with Turkey and Persia. But Atatürk and Reza Shah soon disillusioned them by imprisoning local commu-nists. Hostility was muted, however, by the Soviets' continuing need to have reasonably good relations with states on their frontiers. Turkey and Persia both feared and suspected their northern neighbour's mo-tives, and relations again deteriorated during the Second World War when Stalin laid claim to the eastern provinces of Turkey and invaded northern Persia. The Soviet Union's Arab policy in this period was generally unsuccessful as Moscow could not come to terms with 'bour-geois nationalism', and as Britain and France still had such a strong presence there. After the war the USSR emerged as a more influential power. Stalin, in the flush of victory, while continuing Tsarist policy in Europe by absorbing country after country, also made further demands in the Middle East. He demanded territory in Turkey and the right to garrison troops on the Straits, and in Iran he tried to set up a puppet regime in Azerbaijan. However, both countries, with Anglo-American backing, rebuffed him. In Palestine the Soviets tried to discomfort Britain by backing partition and then by recognizing Israel in 1948. But their policy towards the Arabs was largely one of opportunism.

The first real opening came in 1954–55 when Britain was in the process of trying to establish the Baghdad Pact (which was much resented by many Arabs) and when the United States was about to refuse help to Egypt to construct the Aswan High Dam. The West was also beginning to refuse to arm Nasser's Egypt which meant he had to look elsewhere for sources of aid and arms. The Soviet Union began haltingly to exploit this situation, but had not yet fully realized the military, political and ideological implications of a changing situation. However, Soviet arms began to be delivered to Egypt, through Czechoslovakia, and help was provided to construct the Aswan Dam. The Soviets, having discovered they could do little in Turkey and Persia, or even Israel, leapfrogged over them into the Arab world.

The Soviet Union's opportunity in the region came, particularly in Egypt, when Britain's moment in the Middle East was fast receding in 1956, not least as a result of the Suez War, and while France was engaged in its lengthy struggle against the nationalists in Algeria. The Soviets were able to benefit from the unpopularity of the Western powers, but they had themselves to learn to live with Arab nationalism and the Arab nationalist leaders. There was an uneasy relationship with Abd al-Nasser. Egypt viewed Soviet aid from the perspective of its national self-interest and not on the basis of ideological compatibility. The quarrels between Nasser and Khrushchev were for these very reasons. The Soviet leader resented Nasser's lack of commitment to communism and the fact that he put many Egyptian communists in jail. Nasser resented Khrushchev's heavy-handed attempts to dictate to Egypt. Muhammad Hasanein Haykal, the former Editor of the Cairo daily newspaper *Al-Ahram*, gave an inside picture of this relationship in 1959. Nasser wrote to Khrushchev: 'I am not a Communist. I am a nationalist. But because I attack Communism in the Arab world it should not be taken as a criticism of the Soviet Union'. Khrushchev replied: 'There is a campaign in the United Arab Republic against the Soviet Union and consequently against the Soviet people. Don't spit into the well – you may need the water' (Haykal, 1972, p. 137, 141). By 1960 relations between the two countries were cool although the Soviet Union maintained its commitment to build the Aswan Dam. There were similar difficulties with the Ba'th parties in Syria and Iraq which were also attempting to suppress the local communists in the face of Soviet protests.

In the 1960s the Soviet Union began to formulate a new approach. There was some reappraisal of the Cold War and more stress on peaceful co-existence. Wars, if necessary, could be fought by proxy. A new tactical approach was signalled by the building up of Soviet naval strength in the Mediterranean and in the Indian Ocean. There was a keen awareness of the importance of the Middle East as the area guarding the approaches to the southern Soviet Union. It became more important with the withdrawal of Britain and because the United States could not always fill the gap. There was also a willingness to accept small gains and to work with the peoples of the Middle East rather than to force the blunt approach. Finally, there was a shift in the ideological emphasis. The class struggle was relegated to a secondary position and more stress was laid on the Soviet Union's anti-imperialist, that is, anti-Western, bond with the 'Third World'.

Nevertheless, until a few months before June 1967 there was little evidence of a coherent Soviet policy. Then, after having built up the Syrian and Egyptian armies, all seemed to be in ruins after the disastrous Arab defeat by Israel. Major policy decisions had to be taken. The Soviets under Brzezhnev decided to press ahead on a greater scale. The Arab armies were re-equipped, the Soviet fleet in the area strengthened, base facilities were acquired and thousands of Soviet 'experts' were sent to Arab countries. The years 1967–72 were a period of considerable Soviet presence. Then, to the surprise of many observers, President Sadat began to expel his Soviet advisers. He had become extremely disillusioned with the Soviets who had refused to supply certain weapons to the Egyptian army, who behaved with near contempt towards the Egyptians and who had acquired almost sovereign rights over certain facilities. To Egypt it appeared that the British had been expelled only to be replaced by the Soviets. Sadat gradually turned to America for aid and diplomatic support, a process which led to the US-sponsored Camp David agreement in 1978.

The Soviets followed adventurous policies in several other Middle Eastern countries. In Sudan they had to withdraw when, after being strongly entrenched, the political climate changed. There had to be a similar withdrawal from Somalia. The USSR supported Ethiopia in the war against Somalia where they were largely fighting through the Cuban army. The growing Soviet influence in that area led to fears of Soviet control of the entrance to the Red Sea. And the Soviets were strong backers of the Palestine Liberation Organization (PLO) in its struggle against Israel.

By entering the Middle East the Soviet Union had to counter certain problems and make certain decisions. In supporting particular Arab states it became involved in inter-Arab quarrels. It had to decide whether to support the moderate or the more extreme elements, and whether to come to terms with bourgeois nationalism. Ideology always posed problems. Should the USSR have supported local communist parties even when they were banned by their governments? Finally, there was the difficulty that Moscow could not always deliver the technology that was required by many Middle Eastern countries.

When Gorbachev came to power in 1985 he tried to introduce a new approach into Soviet policy. He was conscious of the dangers of super-power rivalry and nuclear war, and favoured the concept of the balance of interests rather than outright rivalry. He preferred joint action to solve problems and political means to resolve regional conflicts. He stressed the importance of the links between the superpowers and the 'Third World' and at the same time downgraded the importance of the Marxist–Leninist ideology. However, during the period 1979–89, when the Soviet Union was involved in Afghanistan, there seemed to be more continuity than change in Soviet policy, which continued to be largely a reaction to a series of regional developments which Moscow had not caused. But then Gorbachev began to try to limit expensive Soviet involvement in the Middle East.

The biggest 'about turn' was the withdrawal from Afghanistan made after much heart-searching. The continued involvement had been justi-fied by all kinds of casuistic arguments, but basically the invasion took place because of Moscow's desire to control unruly neighbours and to preserve a puppet communist state. The invasion was afterwards quali-fied as an 'aberration' and 'too aggressive', phrases quite unfamiliar in the mouths of Soviet diplomats describing their foreign policy. Then a *rapprochement* was sought with Egypt and President Mubarak, Sadat's more pragmatic successor, and diplomatic relations were established with the Gulf states. Approaches were also made to Saudi Arabia and to Israel, the latter being accompanied by Moscow's policy of allowing Soviet Jews to emigrate.

Since 1989, history has been turned upside down. Soviet policy has come to an end, as has the Soviet Union. Gorbachev has left the scene. A series of agonizing appraisals of past behaviour appeared in the Moscow publication, *International Affairs*, in a report entitled, 'The Foreign Policy and Diplomatic Activity of the USSR', written before the attempted coup. The change of direction was bluntly stated in 1991. There was an advance towards a new world. '[The concept] denotes a stage of transition from a post-war to a new world order under which uncompromising rivalry between the two socio-political systems must give way to partnership and co-operation, to a readiness to renounce force in settling problems arising between them' (Otunbayeva, 1991, p.142).

The article described the Soviet Union as a 'Euro-Asian state' and argued that, 'Russia must live politically in a complex world of both European and Asian peoples'. Moreover, the acknowledgement that 'Russia is destined by history to reconcile, link and merge Europe with Asia in one way or another' (Otunbayeva, 1991 p. 145), reflected more than a touch of the messianic vision. It was admitted, though, that the Soviet Union would have to modify its relations with the Middle East in a situation conditioned by new realities. The Middle East itself would have to review policies which had until then taken advantage of the situation of confrontation. In a statement of amazing historical volte-face the Ministry of Foreign Affairs Survey contended that: 'In 1990 the Soviet Union [was] striving to use political dialogue with [Third World] leaders – the wasteful policy of missionarism must be discarded' (*International Affairs*, Moscow, 1991 p. 46).[3] It was fully recognized that the modification of policy would not be a 'painless process free of friction'[4] and that the 'novelty of our policy expresses itself above all in our attitude towards conflict resolution'.

The positive achievements of Soviet policy were described as the normalization of relations with Egypt, better relations with Saudi Arabia and the establishment of diplomatic ties with Bahrain. Opinions had been exchanged with the PLO, Israel and most Arab nations on how to settle the Palestine issue. A policy of good neighbourliness was expressed towards Turkey, Iran and the Arab world. Iraq had caused the most difficulty when the USSR declined to take Saddam's side in the dispute over Kuwait. 'It was not easy for us to take the stand we took, seeing that we have extensive and manifold ties with Iraq' – but 'we could not have chosen any other course, for there exist principles and norms of international law, such concepts as the inviolability of existing frontiers, respect for the established world order'.[5] Thus was the Soviet Union trying to come in from the cold and seemingly fully recognizing at last that being a world power entailed responsibilities as well as sheer might. But this realization came too late. The pace of change was reflected in the bewilderment of the country's Foreign Ministry statements. The pace quickened as the Soviet Union, the ex-Tsarist Empire, crumbled and the Soviet Foreign Ministry disappeared. Russia has now to establish a new position. Shorn of its republics, which want to follow their own policies, Russia is no longer a superpower but still a great, if suffering, power. There are those who see the future of Russia with the West as a member of NATO, those who see it as a Eurasian power forming the aforementioned link. In between there are those who believe that Russia, because of its size, geography and history, cannot be part of the West, but rather a partner with its own interests which might sometimes differ from those of the West.

Russia is heir to parts of the Soviet Union and retains a voice in world affairs through its seat in the United Nations Security Council. In the Middle East it has inherited both the negative and positive results of earlier Soviet policy. The successes had been to identify, to some extent, with the aspirations of the local people in throwing off the shackles of Western colonialism and to provide aid and support. The failures were the conviction that the world was marching towards socialism with the USSR at its head. Confrontation with the United States stemmed from the beliefs and actions of both sides, and necessarily the Soviets supported those opposed to the Americans. Russia has now officially rejected ideology and confrontation and will pursue a more normal foreign policy. Security will still be of paramount importance within a broader framework of collective security. The southern frontiers, now pushed further north again, will be guarded against possible threats, such as local missiles or a Muslim revival. And Russia will guard against any large American presence to its south.

If ideology is rejected, the basis of foreign policy could then be a sound economic relationship. But Russia will still have a voice in world affairs. Without doubt the debate will continue for years within Russia itself on how to define tomorrow's objectives. The Tsarist–Bolshevik inheritance has been rejected. Russia has now to establish itself on a new footing in its relationship with the rest of the world.

NOTES

1. In 1904 when the Japanese made a surprise attack on Russian ships in the Far East, the Russian Black Sea Fleet was prevented from sailing by the 1841 Convention and the Baltic Fleet had to make the long round-the-world journey. It arrived off the Chinese coast in May 1905 and was decisively defeated.
2. Admiral Sergei Gorshkov, *Pravda*, 26 July 1970.
3. See survey entitled 'The Foreign Policy and Diplomatic Activity of the USSR', prepared by the Ministry of Foreign Affairs, published in the monthly journal *International Affairs* (Moscow) 1991, p. 46.
4. *Ibid.*, p. 47.
5. *Ibid.*, p. 48.

8. The significance of the Madrid peace conference

Avi Shlaim

INTRODUCTION

Since its origins at the end of the 19th century, the Jewish–Arab battle for the possession of Palestine has been accompanied by another battle, fought in the international arena – the battle for hearts and minds of people. Since its origins, the Jewish–Arab conflict has also been an existential conflict between two movements for national liberation, one Jewish and one Palestinian. It was, in essence, a struggle between two peoples for one land. But the Zionists, who led the Jewish struggle for national liberation, deliberately obscured this essence by portraying Palestine as 'a land without a people for a people without a land'.

Zionism is probably the most successful public relations exercise of the 20th century; Palestinian nationalism one of the least successful. At the Middle East peace conference which convened in Madrid in late October 1991 the Palestinians, for the first time ever, began to gain the upper hand in the propaganda battle. It was a historic reversal which could not fail to affect the course of the Israeli–Palestinian conflict in the last decade of the 20th century and beyond.

This chapter examines the reasons behind the apparent shift in the respective fortunes of the protagonists, and analyses the significance of the Madrid conference for the participants and for the American-led peace process which began in the aftermath of the Gulf War.

PROPAGANDA AND THE STRUGGLE FOR PALESTINE

The early Zionists clearly grasped the power of words in the struggle for independence. Theodor Herzl was not a politician but a failed playwright whose book *The Jewish State*, published in 1896, evoked a powerful response among Jews. On 3 September 1897, Herzl wrote in his diary: 'In Basle I founded the Jewish State'. He was referring to the first Zionist Congress which he had convened in Basle. The 'Basle Programme' stated that, 'the aim of Zionism is to create for the Jewish people a home in Palestine secured by public law'. Both the title of Herzl's book and his diary entry suggest that the aim of Zionism, from the start, was an independent Jewish state in Palestine. This long-term aim was deliberately blurred, however, because it would have provoked Arab hostility and been a liability in the struggle to mobilize international support for the establishment of a Jewish national home in Palestine.

Herzl's diary entry highlights a second important aspect of political Zionism, namely the belief that the commitment to an idea and resolutions passed in international gatherings have a crucial role to play in paving the road to statehood. It was precisely because of the military impotence of their movement that the early Zionists set so much store by winning the propaganda battle and mobilizing world-wide the traditional Jewish talents of advocacy and persuasion. They always concentrated their efforts on the leading great power of the day: first it was the Ottoman Turks, then the British and then the Americans.

In order to appeal to public opinion as well as the governments of the great powers, the Zionists cultivated an image of reasonableness and moderation. Their tactics were always flexible even if their long-term aim remained fixed and inflexible. They tended to say 'yes' rather than 'no' to proposals by third parties, even when they had serious reservations about such proposals. Their strategy was a gradualist one. They understood that it was better to take what was on offer at any given time and come back for more later, than to reject it and end up with nothing.

The Zionists accepted in principle nearly all the compromise proposals put forward by Britain for settling the Palestine problem and they enhanced their reputation for reasonableness in the process. They accepted the judgement of Solomon to divide the disputed land between themselves and the Palestinians. When the Peel Commission first proposed in 1937 the partition of Palestine and a tiny Jewish state, the veteran Zionist leader Chaim Weizmann argued that, 'the Jews would be fools not to accept it even if it is the size of a table-cloth'.

The Zionist leaders, especially David Ben-Gurion, were also adept at presenting the Palestinian position in the conflict as unreasonable. It is not that they were not genuinely interested in a compromise solution.

But since the claims of the two sides could not be reconciled, it was preferable that the Palestinians should bear the responsibility for the deadlock.

As far as the public relations aspect of the conflict was concerned, the Zionists were fortunate in having as their opponent Hajj Amin al-Husseini, the Grand Mufti of Jerusalem. For the Mufti epitomized the total rejection of any Jewish claim to Palestine, the all-or-nothing approach, the absolute insistence on rights without any regard for the practical consequences. The Mufti also created a very poor impression abroad by his systematic rejection of all British compromise proposals and by his collaboration with Nazi Germany during the Second World War. In short, the story of the Palestinian struggle for statehood under the British mandate, and the propaganda battle which accompanied it, is the story of the Mufti's ineptitude.

When the United Nations voted for partition in November 1947, showing that the logic of partition had become inescapable, the Zionists accepted the plan with alacrity although a Jewish state within the UN borders would have scarcely been viable. Accepting the resolution of the world body put them within the framework of international legality and provided a charter of legitimacy for the Jewish state. They counted on the Mufti to put himself on the wrong side of the international community by rejecting the UN partition plan, and reject it he did. It was this sophisticated Zionist approach to playing the game of nations which helped them to win a state of their own in 1948, just as the diplomatic inflexibility of the Palestinians helped to bring about the greatest disaster in their history.

PRAGMATISM, OBDURACY AND THE SEARCH FOR LEGITIMACY

Israel and the Palestinians did not change places overnight. The reversal of their strategies and tactics was the result of a gradual process which only reached its climax in Madrid. One landmark in this process was the rise to power in 1977 of the Likud party which rejected the principle of partition, rejected territorial compromise with Jordan and staked a claim to the West Bank as an inalienable part of the Land of Israel. Sinai, which was not part of the Biblical homeland, was traded by Menahem Begin for peace with Egypt despite opposition from right-wing colleagues like Yitzhak Shamir (his successor as Prime Minister).

Another major landmark in this process was the peace offensive launched by the Palestine Liberation Organization (PLO) in 1988. In November of that year the Palestinian National Council (PNC) met in Algiers and accepted the principle of partition and a two-state solution based on all relevant UN resolutions going back to November 1947. The claim to the whole of Palestine was finally laid to rest and a declaration of independence was issued for a mini-state in the West Bank, East Jerusalem and the Gaza Strip.

The passage of these resolutions through the Palestinians' 'parliament' was accompanied by a conscious attempt to project a more moderate image. A special effort was made to gain respectability by dissociating the PLO from international terrorism. PLO Chairman Yasser Arafat made a number of statements on the subject but they failed to satisfy the United States. In the end the United States virtually dictated the text of a declaration which Arafat delivered in Geneva. Although it sounded as if Arafat renounced tourism, what he actually said was 'we absolutely renounce terrorism'. This statement, coming on top of the PNC resolutions, opened the door to the initiation of the dialogue between the PLO and the US government.

By the time the PLO was prepared to accept partition, Israel had changed its mind. Israel's response to the momentous changes that were taking place within the Palestinian camp was a series of 'noes': 'no' to withdrawal from the occupied territories, 'no' to an international conference, 'no' to negotiation with the PLO, 'no' to a Palestinian state. The only positive idea to come out of Israel was Yitzhak Shamir's plan of May 1989 for the holding of elections in the West Bank and in the Gaza Strip, leading to limited autonomy. But Shamir only put forward this idea in response to pressure from Washington and he retreated from it at the first sign of danger that the Palestinians would accept it. Secretary of State James Baker gave a graphic expression of Washington's frustration with Israeli stonewalling by announcing his telephone number and telling the Israelis to call when they were serious about peace.

A major setback in the quest for legitimacy was sustained by the PLO during the Gulf crisis. Frustrated by Israel's rejection of all its peace overtures and the suspension of the dialogue with the US, the PLO recklessly bet on Saddam Hussein and lost. For his own cynical reasons Saddam tried to link Iraqi withdrawal from Kuwait to Israeli withdrawal from the occupied territories. America resisted this linkage on the grounds that the two disputes were unrelated, but it promised to seek a settlement of the Arab–Israeli conflict once the Gulf conflict had been settled. The convening of the Middle East peace conference in Madrid represented the fulfilment of this promise. The 'mother of all battles' threatened by the Iraqi tyrant in the Gulf was followed by the 'mother of all peace conferences' in Madrid.

DIPLOMATIC ROLES REVERSED AT MADRID

What distinguished Madrid from previous Arab–Israeli conferences was that the Palestinians were represented there for the first time on a footing of equality with Israel. Madrid registered the arrival of the Palestinians, long the missing party, at the Middle East conference table. That in itself was a major gain in international recognition. The Palestinians had to pay a stiff price for their ticket of admission to the conference chamber. Even at the level of symbols, so crucial to a movement for national liberation, no concessions were made to them. No Palestinian flag was displayed and no battle fatigues or *keffiyas* were worn in Madrid. All the members of the Palestinian delegation wore smart business suits. As far as dress was concerned, they were indistinguishable from the two former Texas oil men who represented the United States at the talks.

The mere presence of official Palestinian representatives in Madrid marked a change, if not a reversal, of Israel's long-standing refusal to consider the Palestinians as a partner to negotiations, as an *interlocuteur valable*. Israel's veto of members of the PLO and residents of East Jerusalem resulted in a Palestinian delegation which was part of a joint Jordanian–Palestinian delegation and an advisory council, with Faisal al-Husseini as co-ordinator and Dr Hanan Ashrawi as spokeswoman. Ironically, by excluding the PLO, Israel helped the Arabs of the occupied territories to put forward fresh faces. The Palestinian delegation to the conference was the most effective team the Palestinians had ever fielded at an international gathering, and it played the game of nations in Madrid with outstanding skill and flexibility.

The opening speeches by the heads of the Israeli and the Palestinian delegations faithfully reflected the positions of the two sides. Mr Shamir, like the Bourbons of France, seemed to have learnt nothing and to have forgotten nothing. The whole tone of his speech was anachronistic, saturated with the stale rhetoric of the past, and inappropriate for the occasion. He used the platform to deliver the kind of promotional speech for Israel that would normally be heard in an Israel Bonds drive. His version of the Arab–Israeli conflict was singularly narrow and blinkered, portraying Israel simply as the victim of Arab aggression and refusing to acknowledge that any evolution had taken place in the Arab or Palestinian attitude to Israel. All the Arabs, according to Shamir, wanted to see Israel destroyed, the only difference between them was over the way to bring about its destruction. His speech, while long on anti-Arab clichés, was exceedingly short on substance. By insisting that the root cause of the conflict is not territory but the Arab refusal to recognize the legitimacy of the state of Israel, Mr Shamir came dangerously close to rejecting the whole basis of the conference – UN Resolutions 242 and 338 and the principle of land for peace.

The contrast between Mr Shamir's speech and the speech of Dr Haidar Abdul Shafi, the head of the Palestinian delegation, could have hardly been more striking in tone, spirit or substance. This single speech contained more evidence of new thinking than all the other speeches, Arab and Israeli, put together. It was, by any standards, a remarkable speech and its impact was only heightened by the quiet, dignified quality of the delivery. Dr Abdul Shafi reminded the audience that it was time for the Palestinians to narrate their own story. While touching on the past, his speech was not backward-looking but forward-looking. 'We seek neither an admission of guilt after the fact, nor vengeance for past iniquities,' he explained, 'but rather an act of will that would make a just peace a reality.' In the name of the Palestinian people, Dr Abdul Shafi went on:

> We wish to directly address the Israeli people with whom we have had a prolonged exchange of pain: let us share hope instead. We are willing to live side by side on the land and share the promise of the future. Sharing, however, requires two partners willing to share as equals. Mutuality and reciprocity must replace domination and hostility for there to be genuine reconciliation and co-existence under international legality. Your security and ours are mutually dependent, as intertwined as the fears and nightmares of our children.

Dr Abdul Shafi accused Israel of brutal oppression in the occupied territories but he sought to portray the Israelis as fellow victims. 'We have seen you anguish over the transformation of your sons and daughters into instruments of blind and violent occupation,' he said, 'and we are sure that at no time did you envisage such a role for the children whom you thought would forge your future. We have seen you look back in deepest sorrow at the tragedy of your past and look on in horror at the disfigurement of the victim turned oppressor. Not for this have you nurtured your hopes, dreams and your offspring.' This stress on the human cost of occupation, and empathy for the other side, was followed by a handsome tribute to those Israelis who had expressed sympathy and solidarity with the Palestinians.

Dr Abdul Shafi's basic message was that Israeli occupation must be ended, the Palestinians have a right to self-determination, and that they are determined to pursue this right relentlessly until they achieve statehood. The *intifada*, he suggested, had already begun to embody the Palestinian state and to build its institutions and infrastructure. But while staking a claim to Palestinian statehood, Dr Abdul Shafi qualified it in two significant ways. First, he accepted the need for a transitional stage, provided interim arrangements were not transformed into permanent status. Secondly, he envisaged a confederation between an ultimately independent Palestine and Jordan. Dr Abdul Shafi's speech in Madrid was both the most eloquent and the most moderate presentation of the Palestinian case ever made by an official Palestinian spokesman since the beginning of the conflict at the end of the last century. The PLO, for all its growing moderation, had never been able to articulate such a clear-cut peace overture to Israel because of its internal divisions and the constraints of inter-Arab politics. No PLO official had ever been able to declare so unambiguously that a Palestinian state would be ready for a confederation with Jordan. The whole tenor of the speech was more conciliatory and constructive than even the most moderate statements of the PLO. In the words of one PLO official, the speech was 'unreasonably reasonable'.

There was a palpable feeling of history-in-the-making as the soft-spoken doctor from Gaza read his text in the magnificent Hall of Columns in the royal palace in Madrid. Future historians will look back on 31 October 1991 as a landmark in the quest for reconciliation between the national claims of the Palestinians and the Israelis.

The origins of the speech delivered by Dr Abdul Shafi were highly revealing of the strategy adopted by the Palestinian leaders, including the PLO, for the Madrid peace conference. Suggestions that the speech be read in Arabic were turned down on the grounds that it was not intended for the folks back home but the world at large. The main aim of the speech was to counter the harmful stereotypes that have become attached to the Palestinians in world opinion and to humanize the

Palestinian cause. The other aim was to convince the Israeli public that the Palestinians are genuinely committed to peaceful co-existence.

Thirteen drafts of the speech were prepared before consensus was reached on the final text. Dr Hanan Ashrawi, Professor of English literature at Bir Zeit University on the West Bank, was the principal author. She confessed that the speech was written on the assumption that one day it would be taught in primary schools in the state of Palestine. Contributions to the speech were made by fellow Palestinians including Dr Haidar Abdul Shafi, Mamduh Aker, Nabil Shaath (an adviser to Yasser Arafat) and the PLO Chairman himself.

The speech struck just the right note and gave the Palestinians their finest day in Madrid. One Palestinian delegate was even moved to declare, echoing Theodor Herzl nearly a century earlier: 'In Madrid we founded the Palestinian state'. In the international media the speech received every accolade. Even some of the Israeli officials in Madrid professed themselves to be moved by the speech. The calm and reassuring manner of the elderly physician from Gaza only served to underscore the humanity and reasonableness of the message he was bearing.

THE PROPAGANDA BATTLE AT MADRID

Abba Eban's old jibe that the Palestinians 'never miss a chance to miss an opportunity for peace', was singularly inappropriate on this occasion and, if anything, could be turned against the Israeli side. Even the composition of the two delegations was indicative of the historic transformation that had taken place on the road to peace. Half the Palestinian delegates to Madrid were doctors and university professors. The Israeli delegation, on the other hand, was led (as the Syrian Foreign Minister reminded the conference) by a former terrorist who in 1948 was wanted by the British for the assassination of Count Bernadotte, the UN mediator to Palestine. 'This man', he said, brandishing a picture of the 32-year-old Shamir, 'killed peace mediators'.

Shamir's performance in Madrid raised serious questions as to whether he and his generation of Likud party leaders could ever put the past behind them and work towards a genuine accommodation with the Palestinians. Listening to his speech, one Israeli journalist wondered whether his officials had not, by mistake, taken out of their files one of Golda Meir's speeches from the early 1970s. Shamir's basic thesis was that the Arabs still refused to accept Israel as a permanent entity in the Middle East. But the peace with Egypt and the presence in the conference chamber around him of representatives from all the confrontation states, as well as the authorized representatives of the Palestinians, told a completely different story.

The truth is that the Arabs recognized Israel when they signed the armistice agreements with it under UN auspices in Rhodes in 1949 and that there had been countless meetings – some secret, some open – between them and Israel ever since. But Israel continued to claim that the Arabs do not recognize it and to insist on direct negotiations. Some people, it would seem, are never satisfied. After the first day of talks, Mr Shamir was asked how it felt to sit down finally face to face with all Israel's Arab adversaries. He answered: 'It was a regular day'.

Mr Shamir's presence was as much of a liability to the Israeli public relations effort in Madrid as the absence of the PLO was a boon to the Palestinians. In charge of the Israeli public relations effort was Binyamin Netanyahu, then deputy Foreign Minister and now leader of the Likud, who had the advantage of speaking in the short sound-bites beloved by American television interviewers. Mr Netanyahu maintained the highest Israeli profile in the daily battle of the sound-bites waged in Madrid. But he fought a losing battle. As Michael Sheridan wrote in the *Independent* on 2 November 1991:

> The Israelis possessed the best organised, most efficient, least flustered, public relations team at the conference, with Mr Netanyahu, its intellectual bruiser, rushing before the CNN cameras every other minute. But for all its military élan, the Israeli PR machine has without question lost the battle for hearts and minds to the Palestinians this week. Its principal problem was that a million glib sound bites from Mr Netanyahu could not efface the image of Yitzhak Shamir, scowling in repose and truculent in action, a visual epitome of the policy he represents.

Mr Netanyahu was up against Hanan Ashrawi, the spokeswoman of the Palestinian delegation, whose eloquence was matched by patent sincerity and a refreshing habit of answering reporters' questions directly and unambiguously. As spokeswoman, Dr Ashrawi maintained the most visible profile in daily press briefings and numerous interviews to the media. She was clearly the star of the show. Overnight she had become the most prominent woman in the Arab political world. She was every bit as articulate and assertive as the Israelis and considerably more sophisticated in handling the media. To the American public, in particular, she presented an intelligent and sensitive human face and a powerful Palestinian voice.

The Palestinian spokesmen also cut a much more credible figure than the PLO Chairman. The authority of the PLO was never challenged and the delegates from the occupied territories did not set themselves up as an alternative leadership to the PLO. On the contrary, there was very close co-ordination between the Palestinian delegation and the PLO before, during and after the conference. But in Madrid the Arabs of Palestine showed that they have another group of able and authentic leaders who are better qualified to present their case before the tribunal of international public opinion than the discredited leadership in Tunis.

If the Palestinians proved to Shamir that he could no longer rely on them to let him off the hook, he had better luck with Farouk al-Shara, the Foreign Minister of Syria. Al-Shara played the old record of rejectionism and vituperation. He was without doubt the most militant and radical Arab representative in Madrid and he was also the most isolated. The conference degenerated into an unseemly slanging match between the Israeli and the Syrian. Shamir denounced Syria as one of the most repressive and tyrannical regimes in the world. Al-Shara replied in kind, denouncing Israel as a terrorist state led by a former terrorist, and later refused to answer questions at a press conference from Israeli journalists. Against the background of this strident display of Syrian rejectionism, the readiness of the Palestinians to engage in constructive dialogue with the Israelis was all the more striking.

After the plenary session was over, stage two of the peace process began in Madrid. It took the form of a series of separate bilateral meetings between Israel and each of the Arab delegations. Here, too, the Syrians were the most rigid and intransigent whilst the Palestinians seemed more eager than any of the Arab delegations to forge ahead with the talks in order to bring about a freeze on Jewish settlements in the occupied territories. As a result of these differences, the common Arab front collapsed. Syria held out for a unified Arab position to back its demand for an Israeli commitment to trade the Golan Heights for peace before the bilateral talks began. Among the Palestinian delegates there was considerable irritation with Syria's attempt to set an overall Arab agenda in the talks. They broke ranks with Syria and not only held their meeting with the Israelis but shook hands in front of the cameras. What the Palestinians were saying, in effect, was that Syria had no power of veto over their own moves and that they would not allow the 'peace process' with Israel to be held hostage to inter-Arab politics.

THE AMERICAN CONNECTION

Another key to Palestinian success in Madrid was the political alliance they formed with the United States, formally one of the co-sponsors but actually the driving force behind the conference. The whole conference was carefully stage-managed by the Americans with Secretary of State James Baker acting as the chief puppeteer. Despite the unreasonable conditions imposed by Israel, the Palestinians agreed to participate because Mr Baker warned them that this would be their only chance. He also promised them that once the talks were underway, all the pressure would be on Israel to start making concessions.

The emergence of an American–Palestinian axis broke the familiar mould of Middle Eastern politics. Of all the delegations to Madrid, the Palestinians were the only ones who agreed to nearly all the American requests on both procedure and substance. It was the American officials who advised the Palestinians to appeal to the American public, and this advice was followed almost to the point of neglecting public opinion in other countries. In what nearly amounted to a dress rehearsal, the Americans went over different scenarios with the Palestinians before the conference in order to minimize the risk of an Israeli walk-out. The Americans thus had every reason to be pleased with the performance put on by the novices in their début on the international stage in Madrid.

What mattered much more than the polished performance by the novices, was the fact that they were a lot closer than the Israelis to the American position in Madrid. They explicitly accepted that the negotiations should be based on UN Resolutions 242 and 338 and the principle of land for peace, whereas Israel did not. They got on board the bus which Baker told them would come only once, whereas Mr Shamir continued to quibble over the fare, the powers of the driver, the rights of other passengers, the speed of the bus, the route and the final destination.

The reversal of the Palestinian and Israeli positions in relation to American policy in the Middle East carried the most profound historical significance. In the past Israel had been America's principal ally in the Middle East, whereas the Palestinians counted for little in American eyes. 'What about the Palestinians?', John Foster Dulles was asked in 1956. 'Well,' he replied, 'they are unlucky because they fell under the feet of elephants. The old generation will die and the young will forget'. The Palestinians have not forgotten and the then occupant of

Dulles's room in the State Department clearly recognized that the Palestinians could no longer be ignored.

A parallel change was also evident in America's attitude to Israel. The collapse of the Soviet Union as a rival superpower and Saddam Hussein's adventure in Kuwait combined to call into question the special relationship between the United States and Israel. In the past, US aid to Israel, totalling $77 billion, had been justified on the grounds that Israel helped to protect American interests in this vital part of the world against the twin threats of communism and pan-Arab nationalism. But the communist threat had vanished and, when the crucial test came in the war with Iraq, America's much-vaunted strategic asset proved to be an embarrassment and a liability. The best service Israel could render to the United States was to do nothing. George Bush and James Baker, two former Texas oil men not noted for their sentimental attachment to Israel, had no difficulty in reaching the conclusion that America's vital interest lay in cultivating their old and new Arab friends. They were also determined to demonstrate that victory in the Gulf War would pave the way to peace in the Middle East, that although Saddam kept his hold on power, the war had not been in vain.

The official American position towards the Arab–Israeli conflict had remained unchanged since 1967. America supported the exchange of land for peace, refused to acknowledge the Israeli annexation of East Jerusalem and regarded the building of Jewish settlements in the occupied territories as illegal and an obstacle to peace. What changed in the run-up to Madrid was the evident determination of the Bush administration to do more than repeat these positions like a gramophone record. The moderation shown by the Palestinians in Madrid made it easier for the Bush administration to tilt further in their direction and away from Israel. At Madrid the Palestinians were on the side of the most powerful man on earth. As America and the Palestinians became closer, Israel and America began rapidly to drift apart. For the leader of a small state that is so heavily dependent on American support, Shamir behaved in a very odd way. He ignored the golden rule of the leaders of mainstream Zionism: never stage a confrontation with a friendly great power which you cannot hope to win.

Shamir was disturbed by what he described as an increasingly one-sided approach by the United States to the Arab–Israeli conflict. He also felt that he was personally humiliated during his visit to Washington. On 21 November 1991 he came out of a meeting with Mr Baker saying there had been no agreement on the venue and date of the next round of peace talks. He expected to discuss this question at his meeting with President Bush the next day. But before he was able to do so, the Americans formally invited both Israel and the Arabs to Washington to start bilateral talks on 4 December. To make matters worse, the letters of invitation included suggestions on questions of substance designed to narrow the gap between Israel and the Arabs.

The Americans could not afford to lose the momentum of the peace process started in Madrid. They felt they had to keep the pressure on all parties, especially Israel and Syria, to keep moving forward before getting bogged down in the 1992 US presidential election and the Israeli general election. But Mr Shamir and his cabinet colleagues were outraged by America's failure to consult and by its attempt to force the pace. A meeting in the American capital with all the Arab delegations under the same roof on the same day was not their idea of stage two in the peace process. They responded by asking America for a delay of five days to allow more time for consultations and clarifications. Some ministers wanted to withdraw from the talks altogether. Yuval Neeman, the hard-line Minister of Science, suggested sarcastically that the cabinet add a chair for the US ambassador to Israel, so he could give the orders directly. Mr Rechavam Zeevi, a cabinet minister from the rightist Moledet party, claimed that Washington was treating the Israelis like 'the Cherokee tribe of Indians that was put onto a reservation'.[1] Shamir made a series of contradictory statements but was forced to climb down when America held firm on the venue and date of the talks.

The Israeli public did not rally behind Prime Minister Shamir during this confrontation with the Bush administration. Public opinion polls revealed that the Israeli public was much more willing to trade land for peace than was its government. Foreign Minister David Levy, the strongest advocate of the talks within the government, said that Israel was acting 'out of anger rather than logic', and 'treating marginal issues as if they were substantive'. Some members of the opposition privately justified the abrasive behaviour of the Bush administration. Otherwise, they argued, Shamir would pile one delay on top of another. 'On the record? It's horrible what the Americans did', an opposition member of the Knesset said to an American journalist. 'Off the record? I love it. As Woody Allen said, if the end doesn't justify the means, what does?'[2]

The reservations over diplomatic procedure voiced by the Israeli government masked deep-seated unease about the content and direction of the peace process. There was a feeling that the moment of truth was approaching and that Israel would be subjected to mounting pressure to make concessions for peace. Shamir had been suspicious about this process from the start. The last thing he wanted was the kind of brisk and concrete down-to-business approach urged by the Americans. A past master at playing for time, he resorted to all his familiar tricks of obstinacy, obfuscation and procrastination. While calling repeatedly for direct negotiations between Israel and the Arabs, Shamir continued to erect obstacles on the path to negotiations. The gap between the declaratory level and the operational level of his foreign policy had grown so wide that it was difficult to avoid the conclusion that his real aim was to scuttle the peace talks in a way for which the Arabs could be blamed.

CONCLUSION

Since 1948 Israel's leaders, of all political complexions, had never ceased to proclaim their readiness to meet the Arabs anywhere, at any time, to discuss peace. When Golda Meir was Prime Minister, even her officials tired of hearing the refrain repeated. Some of them even joked about Golda's laundrette which was open 24 hours a day. But after the Madrid conference the moment of truth had arrived. Israel's leaders could no longer hide behind the claim that there was no one to talk to on the other side.

Whatever history's verdict on Prime Minister Shamir's role in the Madrid peace talks, his behaviour amply demonstrated that the rejectionist boot was now firmly on the other foot. The Israeli position as presented by Shamir was not only intransigent but seen to be intransigent. The Palestinians, on the other hand, appeared to have learnt a great deal from the mistakes of their leaders and from the success of their opponents, and to have distilled new wisdom from past experience. Foremost among the lessons they learnt were the value of good public relations, the importance of not staking out maximalist positions, the advantage of saying 'yes, but' rather than saying 'no', and the virtue of a gradualist approach. Above all, the Palestinians clearly recognized at last the value for a weak national liberation movement of having a powerful sponsor when playing the rough and cruel game of international politics.

Since the historic meeting in Madrid, the peace process has encountered severe challenges and met with only limited success. Arab and world reactions to Israel's brutal treatment of Palestinian militants has been one complicating factor. The challenge of Hamas to the PLO, and the challenge of Jewish settlers in the occupied territories to the Jewish state, further demonstrate the fragility of even the most lauded developments in the search for peace in the Middle East – the conclusion of a limited peace agreement between Israel and the PLO in September 1993, and the subsequent achievement of limited Palestinian autonomy in Jericho and the Gaza Strip in May 1994. Such problems threaten the positive outcomes of a process, begun at Madrid, which has been widely seen as a watershed in the history of the Israeli–Palestinian conflict. At Madrid and subsequently, the Palestinians not only demonstrated a capacity for moderation, but were seen to be moderate. Perhaps this was the most encouraging outcome of all. If, despite everything, the Palestinians adhere to this quintessentially Zionist strategy, they may well end with a state of their own – just like the Zionists.

NOTES

1. Jackson Diehel, 'Israeli Ministers, Denouncing US, Stand by Shamir', *International Herald Tribune*, 2 December 1991.
2. Clyde Haberman, 'Israeli Officials Spell Out Conditions for Agreeing to Washington Talks', *International Herald Tribune*, 26 November 1991.

Bibliography

al-Asad, H. (1986a), in Qurneh, A. (ed.), *Hafiz al-Asad: Mawsu'a Kamila 1970–1985*, Pt. 4, Aleppo: Dar al-Sharq al-'Arabi.

al-Asad, H. (1986b), 'Al-Dawla al-Asriyya [The Modern State]', in Qurneh, A. (ed.), *Hafiz al-Asad: Mawsu'a Kamila 1970–1985*, Pt. 2, Aleppo: Dar al-Sharq al'Arabi.

al-Jabari, M.A. (1993), 'Ashkaliyya al-Dimuqratiqqa w-al-Mujtama' al-Madani fi al-Watan al-'Arabi', *Al-Mustaqbal al-'Arabi'*, **167** (1).

al-Khafaji, I. (1986), 'State Incubation of Iraqi Capitalism', *MERIP Report*, 142.

Allen, J.A. and Mallat, C. (eds) (1995), *Water in the Middle East*, London: I.B. Tauris.

al-Sayyid, M.K. (1993), 'A Civil Society in Egypt?', *Middle East Journal*, **47** (2), Spring.

Bagis, A.I. (1989), *GAP: Southeastern Anatolia Project, the Cradle of Civilisation Regenerated*, Istanbul: Interbank.

Buzan, B. (1992), 'New Patterns of Global Security in the Twenty-first Century', *International Affairs*, **67** (3), July.

Carr, O. (1985), 'Introduction', in Carr, O. and Dumont, P. (eds), *Radicalismes Islamiques* **1**, Paris: L'Harmattan.

Collins, R.O. (1990), *The Waters of the Nile: Hydropolitics and the Jonglei Canal 1900–1988*, Oxford: Clarendon.

Dann, U. (1969), *Iraq under Qassem*, New York: Praeger.

Deng, F.M. (1990), 'War of Visions for the Nation', *Middle East Journal*, **44** (4), Autumn.

Farouk-Sluglett, M. (1993), 'The Meaning of "Infitah" in Iraq', *Review of Middle East Studies*, **6**.

Foreign and Commonwealth Office (1990), *The Nile Waters*, Foreign Policy Document No. 210.

Foster, E. and Hollis, R. (1991), *War in the Gulf: Sovereignty, Oil and Security*, London: RUSI Whitehall Paper Series No. 8.

Gilbert, F. (ed.) (1975), *The Historical Essays of Otto Hintze*, New York: Oxford University Press.

Guariso, G. and Whittington, D. (1987), 'Implications of Ethiopian Water Development for Egypt and Sudan', *Water Resources Development*, **3** (2).

Haykal, M.H. (1972), *Nasser: The Cairo Documents*, London: New English Library.

Hintze, O. (1975) in Gilbert, F. (ed.), *The Historical Essays of Otto Hintze*, New York: Oxford University Press.

Hopwood, D. (1969), *The Russian Presence in Syria and Palestine 1843–1914*, London: Oxford University Press.

Howell, P., Lock, M. and Cobb, S. (eds) (1989), *The Jonglei Canal: Local Impact and Opportunity*, Cambridge: Cambridge University Press.

Hussein, Saddam (1987–1990), *Al- Mu'allafat al-Kamila*, Pt.15, Baghdad: Dar al-Shu'un al-Taqafiyya al-'Amma.

Kienle, E. (1990), *Ba'ath v. Ba'ath: The Conflict Between Syria and Iraq 1968–1989*, London: I.B. Tauris.

Krishna, R. (1995), 'International Watercourses: World Bank Experience and Policy', in Allan, J.A. and Mallat, C. (eds) *Water in the Middle East*, London: I.B. Tauris.

Nasr, S. (1985), 'Mobilisation Communautaire et Symbolique Religieuse: l'imam Sadr et les Chi'tes du Liban 1970–75', in Carr, O. and Dumont, P. (eds), *Radicalismes Islamiques*, **1** Paris: L'Harmattan.

Norton, A.R. (1993), 'The Future of Civil Society in the Middle East', *Middle East Journal*, **47** (2), Spring.

Otunbayeva, R. (1991), 'On the Threshold of a New World Order', *International Affairs* (Moscow), **1** (4).

Parker, M. (1991), 'Rumbles in the Peace Pipeline', *South*, **124**, August.

Pearce, F. (1991), 'Wells of Conflict on the West Bank', *New Scientist*, 1 June.

Perthes, V. (1992), 'The Syrian Economy in the 1980s', *Middle East Journal*, **46** (1), Winter.

Qurneh, A. (ed.) (1986), *Hafiz al-Asad: Mawsu'a Kamila 1970–1985*, Aleppo: Dar al-Sharq al-'Arabi.

Ramazani, R.K. (1992), 'Iran's Foreign Policy: Both North and South', *Middle East Journal*, **46** (3), Summer.

Roberts, A. (1992), 'A New Age in International Relations', *International Affairs*, **67** (3), July.

Schofield, R.N. (1991), *Kuwait and Iraq: Historical Claims and Territorial Disputes*, London: RIIA.

Schofield, R.N. (ed.) (1993), *Territorial Foundations of the Gulf States*, London: UCL Press.

Seale, P. (1988), *Asad: The Struggle for the Middle East*, London: I.B. Tauris.

Shahin, M. (1985), *Hydrology of the Nile Basin*, Amsterdam: Elsevier.

Shuval, H.I. (1992), 'Approaches to Resolving the Water Conflicts Between Israel and Her Neighbours: A Regional Water-for-Peace Plan', *Water International*, **17**.

Tahal, Y. (1990), *Israel Water Sector Review*, New York: World Bank.

United Nations (1992), *Water Resources of the Occupied Palestinian Territories*, Report prepared for the Committee on the Exercise of the Inalienable Rights of the Palestinian People, New York: United Nations.

Vandewalle, D. (1991), 'Qadhafi's "Perestroika" – Economic and Political Liberalization in Libya', *Middle East Journal*, **45** (2), Spring.

Walker, J. (1993), 'Practical Problems of Boundary Delimitation in Arabia: The Case of the United Arab Emirates', in Schofield, R.N. (ed.), *Territorial Foundations of the Gulf States*, London: UCL Press.

Waterbury, J. (1979), *Hydropolitics of the Nile Valley*, Syracuse: Syracuse University Press.

Wilson, R. (ed.) (1991), *Politics and the Economy in Jordan*, London: Routledge.

Index

Abdullah, Sheikh and Transjordan 63
Abu Musa 15, 55–7
Aden 62, 66
  border with Yemen 65
Afghanistan
  and Soviet Union 118, 130
  and Tsarist Russia 121, 123
Aker, Mamduh 140
al-Asad, Hafiz 26, 48, 101, 102
al-Husseini, Hajj Amin (Grand
    Mufti) 135
al-Nasser, Gamal Abd 15, 101, 128
al-Salim, Sheikh Ali Sabah 44–5
al-Shara, Farouk 142
Algiers agreement (1975) 112
Aoun, General 101
Arab–Israeli dispute 38–9
  and post-Gulf War diplomacy
    135–42
  and role of propaganda 133–5
  role of United States in 143–6
  water issues in 83–7
  see also Israel; Jordan; Palestine;
    Palestine Liberation Organi-
    zation; Syria
Arab Revolt 62
Arab states
  and frontier delimitation 61–72
  political regimes in 22–30
  political trends in 17–36
  social structures of 19–22
  state structures of 30–33
Arabian Peninsula
  Arab territorial changes in 63
  and conflict in 92–3, 101
  and discovery of oil 66–7
  economic success of 101, 103
  and Great Britain 62
  and oil wealth 102

  and Oman borders 62
Arafat, Yasser 136, 140
  see also Palestine Liberation
    Organization
Armenia 121
  and Iran 114
Ashrawi, Dr Hanan and Madrid
    peace conference 137, 140,
    141–2
Aswan High Dam 75, 127, 128
  and Egyptian–Sudanese Agree-
    ment 75
Ataturk Dam 80
Ataturk, Kemal 65, 127
Austria and Tsarist Russia 121
Azerbaijan 127
  and Iran 112, 113–14
  see also Stalin, Joseph; Tsarist
    Russia
Aziz, Tariq 101

Baghdad Pact 127
Bahonar, Ayatollah 108
Bahrain
  and defence pact with Britain 55
  and dispute with Qatar 72
  and Gulf Co-operation Council 37,
    49
  and security policy 46
Baker, James 16, 144
  and Arab inequalities 103
  and Madrid peace conference
Balfour Declaration 62
Baltic Sea 115, 119
Ba'th party 12, 91, 93, 128
  see also Iraq; Saddam Hussein;
    Syria
Begin, Menachem 135
Beheshti, Ayatollah 108